MANPOWER STRATEGY
FOR
DEVELOPING COUNTRIES

Lessons from Ethiopia

Manpower Strategy for Developing Countries

LESSONS FROM ETHIOPIA

✦

by

ELI GINZBERG

and

HERBERT A. SMITH

✦

COLUMBIA UNIVERSITY PRESS · 1967 · NEW YORK AND LONDON

To my friends on Martha's Vineyard
For the pleasure of their company.

After the sun has moved beyond Weckman's garden
And Walter has left for home
And I have finished my writing for the day.

Foreword

THIS BOOK is an enlarged version of a report entitled *A Manpower Strategy for Ethiopia*, which was prepared for the government of Ethiopia under the auspices of the United States Agency for International Development. The investigation was carried out during the first half of 1966; the report was completed in July and was printed in Addis Ababa in November.

Several readers of the early report recommended that it be made more generally available since its approach was apposite to analyzing the manpower of a great many developing countries. In responding to the suggestion, I added at the end of each chapter, except the first, a few pages to point up the relevance for other countries of the lessons that can be extracted from the experience of Ethiopia.

Mr. Willard Meinecke, who was director of USAID, Ethiopia, during the course of our investigation, and the members of his staff, and His Excellency Getahun Tessema, the Minister of National Community Development, and the members of his staff, provided a wide range of assistance which made it possible for us to learn a great deal in a short period and to develop perspective in interpreting what we learned.

Ruth S. Ginzberg styled the tables and edited the manuscript for press.

ELI GINZBERG
Director, Conservation of
Human Resources Project

Columbia University
January, 1967

Contents

1	WHAT IS A MANPOWER STUDY?	1
2	THE SHAPING INSTITUTIONS	11
3	STRATEGIC MANPOWER ISSUES	31
4	TRANSFORMING THE SUPPLY	45
5	THE STRUCTURE OF DEMAND	70
6	UTILIZATION	90
7	EDUCATION AND MANPOWER	109
8	LEVERAGES	133
9	THE LONGER VIEW	152
10	THE NEXT STEPS	167
	INDEX	183

MANPOWER STRATEGY
FOR
DEVELOPING COUNTRIES

Lessons from Ethiopia

✦ 1 ✦

What Is a Manpower Study?

ALTHOUGH the early economists knew that the dexterity and skill of the population is a major determinant of the wealth of a nation, the systematic study of manpower has been undertaken only recently. The study of manpower as a field emerged with the manpower stringencies that characterized the nations involved in World War II. A further stimulus to the development of the field has been the widespread concern and efforts in the last two decades to speed the economic development of many old and new nations. While statesmen and economists believed initially that the pace of development was primarily if not solely a matter of capital inputs, it soon became clear that the competence and skill of a nation's people are important in determining the rate of development.

Since manpower analysis had its origins in economics, and since economic analysis has become increasingly quantitative during the past several generations, it is not surprising that many students of manpower have sought to approach their subject solely along a quantitative axis. They have sought to determine the present demand for various types of skills and to compare this with the num-

bers of trained persons available. This comparison provides a set of surpluses and shortages.

Next they estimate the demand for different types of
skill that may prevail at some time in the future, against
which they set the present supply and the number of those
in training, less an estimated number of those who will retire or die, and thus establish a net balance for the target
date. With this information they can see where skills are
likely to be in oversupply or in deficit. By recommending
policies aimed at altering the flow of persons into certain
types of training, they hope to avoid prospective shortages
or overages. A great many manpower studies in recent
years, both in developed and developing societies, have followed this model. Sometimes the estimates of present and
future demand and supply are gross, sometimes they are
more detailed. Sometimes the analytical apparatus is simple, sometimes it is sophisticated. But in no instance can
the results transcend the approach itself.

This simplistic approach has inherent defects. The most
serious relate to the determination of future demand. One
characteristic of an evolving society is that it alters the way
in which goods and services are produced. There is con-
stant pressure on employers to increase their productivity
by altering the composition of their inputs. This pressure
is increased whenever there are shortages of skill which
force employers to search for alternative inputs. They may
substitute a less scarce type of manpower or increase the
proportion of capital to labor. When any of these circumstances occur, projections based on current ratios of skilled
manpower to output will prove faulty.

There are other difficulties in projecting demand in developing countries. When estimates of the future need for
skill are based on the translation of development plans
into manpower terms, they will prove correct only when

the development plans themselves are implemented and within the time period specified. The weight of the evidence is overwhelming, however, that developing, in fact even developed, countries are not regularly able to match execution with plan. The deviations from the plan are usually substantial, particularly among developing nations which are just gaining experience in economic planning.

Among the reasons for the gaps between intention and execution are unexpected shortages of professional, technical, and skilled manpower. A shortfall in output is often centered in a lack of competence. If a plan's major targets are not fulfilled, estimates of future manpower requirements will be awry.

So far we have dealt with the future demand for manpower as an entity, but a development plan is a composite of a great number of discrete sectors—agriculture, construction, manufacturing, services—which in turn are built up from many subcomponents. While gross estimates about the future are difficult, estimates about the individual sectors and subsectors that comprise the whole are even more complicated. From a manpower point of view, however, the detailed information is frequently most important. If the plan provides for a fertilizer factory, the estimates of manpower requirements will include a certain number of chemical and electrical engineers and technicians. But if the plan is altered, if the fertilizer factory is not built and a road program is expanded instead, the requirement will be for civil engineers. In the event of an unexpected shortage in food production, funds may have to be diverted to importing additional food so that neither the factory nor the roads are built. In that case the entire trained manpower requirement evaporates.

In sophisticated hands, gross calculations about the scale and scope of the investment program can be used as a rough guide to the levels of future demand for certain broad categories of manpower. As such it can be one useful if limited tool in an armamentarium of manpower planning. But there is no justification for using an investment program as the sole or even primary basis for calculating in detail the future requirements for different types of skill.

A brief word about the major alternative approach generally used to the thorny problem of estimating future requirements. This approach, used in both developed and developing nations, involves asking employers about their estimates of future requirements for various numbers and types of professional, technical, and skilled workers. Sometimes the coverage is broad, sometimes it is limited to a small sample. Sometimes the inquiry is by mail, sometimes by interview. But these are minor differences. The important facts are, first, that each employer responds in terms of his own judgment about the future trend of business in general and his business in particular; second, the longer the time period the less valid his forecasts will be; and finally, there tends to be a strong optimistic bias in all such estimates. This approach should not be relied upon except for very short-run forecasts, and even then caution must be exercised in its use.

The quantitative approach has equally important limitations when it is used to forecast supply. In general, forecasts start with an assumption that the reporting system covering professional and skilled manpower by occupational categories is comprehensive and revelatory. But no country in the world has good occupational data. Moreover, the range of competence among members in the same group is frequently substantial. There is little value in knowing that a developing nation has 500 engineers unless one knows how many of this 500 have the knowledge, skill, flexibility, and other qualifications which would enable them to work successfully on a contemplated new project. While considerations of numbers are relevant, in matters of professional and skilled manpower, considerations of quality are even more relevant.

In the more advanced sectors of an economy, no man, no matter what his level of skill, works alone. Therefore in manpower studies we must allow for the fact that under pressure people will be able to handle a higher level of work. Many a technician today carries on work which calls for an engineer. And conversely, many engineers today are working below a professional level either because technicians are not available or because they themselves are not capable of working on a professional level. All estimates of supply are contaminated by this blurring at the margins of the occupational hierarchy.

In addition, men trained in one field frequently work in another. Flexibility is an outstanding characteristic of trained men. A mathematician may in fact be employed as a production manager. A chemist may run a sales agency. A teacher may become a tax official. The more training a man has the more likely it is that he will be able to shift to a new field if the opportunity offers. Shortages imply opportunities. Therefore they are frequently overcome not by people especially trained for the field but by competent individuals transferred from another field. Most manpower estimates do not allow adequately for this pervasive phenomenon.

From what has been said we can deduce what a manpower study is not. It is not a balance of present supplies, plus the numbers in the pipeline, minus those who will retire or die, yielding a future net supply which is then juxtaposed against one or another estimate of future requirements based on data derived from the national plan, employers' estimates, or other guidelines. While such an approach may have some value in establishing limits for gross categories of manpower, depending on the ready availability of planning data, it is only the beginning of a sound inquiry.

What, then, is a manpower study and how can one carry one out so that it has validity and usefulness? A first approach is to become familiar with the economy and society as it currently is and as it is likely to develop in order to identify present and potential areas of manpower stringency. This does not imply a listing of all the types of trained people who are in short supply in terms of those required to provide basic services to the population, such as teachers, physicians, nurses, engineers, agronomists, or those needed to speed the expansion of the modern industrial and commercial sector, such as qualified managers, accountants, and production and marketing specialists. Such a listing would have little point since the specified manpower deficiencies would not necessarily be related to the ability of the society to employ such people if they could be trained. Developing nations are poor nations, and they lack not only trained manpower but a great many other essentials to speed economic and social expansion: capital, markets, infrastructure—in fact, they are likely to be handicapped in varying degrees along each of these fronts.

Therefore, the reconnoitering of the society to identify continuing pressure areas where the supply and demand of skills is out of balance must be in accord with the scale and scope of possible action by employers, government and non-government alike. One must seek to determine the areas where ongoing and development programs have been retarded because of employers' difficulties in attracting and retaining adequate numbers of properly qualified persons.

Toward this end, there are several clues. First, the salary

structure. If a developing nation provides a markedly higher salary for a graduate engineer than for a graduate in public administration, this is presumptive evidence that engineers are currently more scarce. The rate of replacement of foreigners by the local population or the number of new work permits issued to foreign specialists provides another clue to areas of current skill stringency. A review of the changing numbers of people in the training pipeline, both those studying at home and those pursuing their education abroad, may prove suggestive. Another indicator is the placement experience of recent graduates. For instance, have prospective employers been competing avidly for certain types of specialists while showing only limited interest in others? Another clue is the extent to which employers, faced with acute shortages of professional and technical manpower, have sought to develop up-grading schemes or institute special training programs for subprofessional personnel.

An informed probing of recent manpower developments is a useful first orientation. But that is all it is. It may help the investigator to differentiate the more important from the less important facets of the problem.

Since in developing nations a very high proportion of the total population lives on the land, anchored in a subsistence economy, with little or no access to schooling, a manpower study is likely to focus on the more dynamic urban sector where people with varying orders of education and skill live and are employed. This is the preferred initial focus, although linkages must be made to the large rural population. Slowly or rapidly, schools will penetrate the countryside; slowly or rapidly, the younger, more active, part of the rural population will begin to drift to the cities; development will begin to alter the subsistence economy, creating a demand for goods, services, and trained people in the countryside. Since the majority of the population lives on the land, this sector contains a high proportion of the total human potential of the nation. This fact can be ignored only at the price of slowing national progress.

We see, then, that a manpower study in a developing nation must begin by sorting out and assessing the problems connected with the acquisition of skill and competence and the effective employment of trained persons, but it cannot long ignore the relation between this small superstructure and the large base of uneducated rural population that must sooner or later be caught up.

There are some additional guidelines that should be delineated. The first relates to the interrelations between the number and quality of trained personnel. The number of educated and trained people is likely to be related to the number who show high orders of competence. If a new university has twenty faculty members with a doctorate, it is more likely to have two or three men with substantial strength than if it has only five with a doctorate. In considering professional and skilled manpower, one must be concerned not only with the total number of qualified persons but particularly with the number of truly able people who can cope successfully with the more complex problems that the emerging society faces. Here is a further reason to move cautiously when following a quantitative approach. Distinctions of quality are often of overriding significance.

Another useful distinction in manpower planning is between the short-run and the long-run and particularly the relations between the two. The problems of life cannot be postponed. They must be met as they arise. Therefore it is urgent to adapt the limited trained manpower available to high priority requirements. The expansion of the school system cannot always wait until an adequate cadre of properly qualified teachers has been trained. Compromises and improvisations must be made. But the imperatives of the short-run should not be permitted to go unchallenged.

A developing nation must also be concerned about its future and about the steps that it must take today to expand and improve its supply of trained manpower to meet its future needs. The more a nation understands the ways in which the manpower structure can be influenced, the better its prospects of adopting policies that will optimize the balances that must be made between the short run and the long run, between expediency and standards, between numbers and quality.

Basic to this understanding is a knowledge of the way in which different parts of the manpower structure are interrelated. For instance, while the formal educational system carries primary responsibility for the development of skill, an earlier critical role is played by the family and the community in instilling values and attitudes toward study and work. Similarly, it is important to recognize that much skill is acquired outside of the formal educational system in specialized institutions such as the military, and through on-the-job training and self-development efforts.

A common error in both developing and developed nations is to focus exclusively on matters of manpower supply and to give short shrift to considerations of manpower utilization. But underemphasis or neglect of utilization is an error since a trained person who is not used or who is only poorly used is not really an asset. Manpower analyses must pay particular attention to utilization, since improvements on this front offer one of the best prospects of securing a better balance between a limited supply of and an unmet demand for skill.

The effectiveness of a manpower study is the extent to which it uncovers critical points where policy can impinge to secure a better result. Facts, figures and understanding may be interesting and illuminating, but every country needs much more from research. It needs information from the specialists as to how their findings can be used to bring about a more effective use of scarce human resources so that the society can move more speedily toward the realization of its goals. The test of a manpower study is the new guidelines which it can draw for policy in such important areas as education, training, wage structures, and utilization. But even a successful manpower study is only one stage in a continuing process.

The facts, figures, and interpretations that are made at one point in time may suggest new directions for policies and illuminate the weakness of others. But the results of any study soon become obsolescent. The challenge to every society, developing and developed alike, is to provide a continuing mechanism for the systematic study of its evolving manpower requirements and supply so that it can continuously assess the policies that it is pursuing to develop and utilize more effectively this most valuable of all its resources.

✦ 2 ✦

The Shaping Institutions

MORE THAN a half century ago the great German sociologist, Max Weber, first propounded his thesis that the acceleration of business enterprise in western and northern Europe was directly associated with the value transformations that accompanied the rise of Protestantism. In Weber's opinion, the new stress on individualism, rationality, and salvation through work was basic to unleashing the forces out of which modern capitalism was born. It is not necessary to argue whether Weber was right in most or all respects or whether he exaggerated the linkages between changes in religious and other values and changes in economic performance. But this much is clear: linkages exist in every society between the dominant traditions and folkways and the ways in which a people commit their time and energy to the pursuit of dominant goals. No manpower study can remain oblivious to the more important of these linkages.

The manpower specialist must have a perceptive understanding of the history and culture of the nation he is studying; otherwise he may overlook important determinants or give incorrect weights to those which he singles

out for special consideration. But he must select the determinants; his effort can be improved or corrected by those
who are more knowledgeable. He must not remain silent
on what may be critically important in the development
and utilization of the nation's manpower resources.

We will set forth briefly three sets of considerations: the
basic geographic, climatic, and historical forces that have
helped to shape Ethiopia; the significant changes that have
occurred since its liberation from Italian occupation when
the Emperor returned from exile, which have a direct
bearing on the development and utilization of the nation's
human resources; and finally, certain key data about the
changing economy. We will conclude with a few comments
about the direction of future developments.

Ethiopia is an ancient kingdom whose traditions for the
most part have been transmitted orally. With the exception of a small group of ecclesiastics and a few members of
the principal families, illiteracy has been the rule. Recent
research on the relation between education and economic
development makes the important point that as far as the
Western world is concerned, the establishment of a fairly
high level of literacy—of the order of one-third of the
population—was a precondition for the expansion of commercial and later industrial capitalism. The same finding
appears to hold for other economies such as those of the
Soviet Union and modern Japan.

The topography of Ethiopia, with its high inland pla-
teaus, helps to explain why invaders from the north and
east were repeatedly repulsed. But while the sheltered
nature of the terrain provided a powerful defense, it also
carried a price. Ethiopia was substantially cut off from the
main streams of trade. We know that the diffusion of technology and the dynamizing of an economy is greatly
affected by the ease with which a people can come into fre-

quent contact with other peoples, near and far. The extent
of Ethiopia's isolation is suggested by the observation that
the wheel first became familiar to many Ethiopians within
the past decade when Ethiopian Airlines started a domestic
service.

Another characteristic of the topography may help to
explain why so many Ethiopians do not use wheels. The
high plateau is cut by very deep gorges which greatly limit
communications. Only man or mule can negotiate the
steep descents and ascents and then only at great cost in time
and energy. One senior government official recently estimated that about 60 percent of the Ethiopian population
today lives more than a half-day by mule away from a good
weather road. Another estimate is that only 8 percent of
the land area of Ethiopia is within a half-day by mule from
a good weather road. It is not rare to hear about people
riding eight hours by horseback to reach a community, or
even spending eight days walking from one settlement to
another.

Topography can help explain certain other important
characteristics of the country and its history. While the
Amharas are the dominant people in the upland plateau,
different tribes with distinctive languages and customs are
found throughout the country. The successful joining of
the Amharas with these other tribes into a nation was not
achieved until the nineteenth century under the leadership of emperors Theodorus and Menelik, and the maintenance and strengthening of these national ties has been
one of the great challenges and successes of the present
emperor, Haile Selassie I.

We have noted that the vast majority of the population
is nonliterate; in addition, the persistence of a great many
tribal languages places a formidable hurdle in the path of
speeding the education of the Ethiopian population. Since

Amharic is only now being modernized and may only in the future include the vocabulary requisite for dealing with the abstractions of modern thought, English has been established as the basic language of instruction in the post-elementary schools. This means that everybody who aspires to more than a basic education must learn English. School children who come from non-Amharic–speaking homes and communities face a double challenge: first, to learn Amharic, the language of the nation and the lower school, and second, to acquire a mastery of English. These language difficulties cannot be overestimated in assessing the problems that Ethiopia confronts as it seeks to speed education and develop a more skilled and competent population.

Topography also plays an important part in determining the patterns of land ownership and land use—the foundation of the country's economy. There are a great many different systems of land tenure in effect and many experts believe that an increase in agricultural output hinges on reforms that will assure the tenants a sufficiently large share of any additional output to stimulate their making the extra effort. A new Ministry of Land Reform has recently been established which indicates the importance that the government has come to attach to this subject.

Other aspects of land holding and land cultivation stemming out of the past warrant brief attention. Emperor Menelik gave substantial tracts of land to both priests and officers in lieu of wages. But the children of priests did not always become priests, and currently soldiers receive pay. Hence much of the land has come to be the private property of individuals through inheritance, and many of them are absentee landlords.

Much of the land is held communally and it is often very difficult if not impossible for a farmer to reap benefits from special efforts that he might be willing to expend. In brief, the system of land ownership and cultivation is poorly adapted to the imperatives of a money economy.

Because the overwhelming proportion of the Ethiopian population lives in rural communities, and because it is estimated that about two-thirds of the Gross National Product of E$2.5 billion originates in agriculture, a few more remarks about land and agriculture may be helpful.* There is some virgin land in Ethiopia, mostly in the lowlands in the south. Excessively hot weather during certain periods of the year, the prevalence of malaria, and the absence of roads have retarded settlement on these good lands. Now, however, programs are under way to control and eradicate malaria. The population to land ratio in the north, which has become less favorable, is also exerting pressure on the population to move and settle in the south. The extent and speed with which Ethiopia succeeds in expanding its agricultural output may be more closely linked with settlement of these virgin lands than with an increase in the productivity of the plateau lands.

Although Ethiopia has had substantial protection from foreign invaders because of its topography, it suffered from unsettled internal conditions through many centuries. Warfare was a way of life for many tribes, and soldiers lived off the farmers. Farmers had little incentive to raise more than they required for their own immediate needs since they were exposed to the extortions of both the soldiers who protected them and those who attacked them. This has left its mark on the attitudes of the Ethiopian farmer toward work and accumulation. His has been a subsistence orientation.

Soldiers were not the only ones who helped themselves;

* All figures in this report are in Ethiopian dollars; E$1 equals $.40 U.S.

so did many others in a position of authority and power. Even today it is reported that migratory workers who earn reasonably good wages picking coffee tend to spend all of their earnings before returning to their villages because they fear that any savings may be extracted from them by those in power. Rapid economic development has always required strong government, rule by law, and an honest officialdom. Every developing country must establish these preconditions.

For centuries, service in the church and the army were the most honored of professions. Trade and crafts were looked down upon if not despised by the dominant Amharas. It is not surprising, therefore, that foreigners came to control the more important sectors of commerce and that foreigners and members of some of the less prestigious tribes comprised most of the small number of craftsmen. Leading Amharas were found in the army, the church, and more recently in the expanding government bureaucracy.

The church here refers to the Coptic church, to which most Amharas and many of the other tribes adhere. However, Ethiopia also has a significant number of Muslims in the north, east, and southeast, as well as a significant minority of Animists, mostly on the western border. Ethiopia therefore has to contend not only with many tribal groups speaking different languages, but must also take into account significant differences in religious beliefs.

Note should be taken of the long-time presence in the country of various missionaries who, in addition to seeking converts, were responsible for the establishment of some of the earliest schools and medical facilities and who thereby made a small but significant contribution to the training of the initial cadre of skilled manpower. Present regulations provide that missionaries are permitted to work in the country only if they pursue, in addition to their religious goals, educational, health, or other socially valuable activities.

So much for the continuing influence of the past on the present. Attention will now be focused on certain important developments stemming from the Occupation. Here, in brief, was the Italian legacy: they killed a great many patriots, particularly those in the younger age groups, who normally would have assumed leadership posts in the 1950s and 1960s. An entire generation is missing. But the Italians did leave a much expanded arterial road system. They also trained a limited number of Ethiopians in basic skills. Moreover, they had earlier developed Eritrea, which officially became a province of Ethiopia in 1963. Finally there were a large number of skilled Italian civilians in the country at the time of the Italian military withdrawal. One of the Emperor's first orders upon his return was to protect these civilians. In this way, he insured that their skills would not be lost to his country. Italians have played a leading role in many developing sectors of the economy, particularly in construction.

After his return, the Emperor intensified his efforts to strengthen the national government, an undertaking which had been central to his planning ever since he first came to power. Traditionally, the national government had provided very little by way of direct services to the population. However, after the liberation, the Emperor inaugurated a major effort on the educational front, emphasizing his interest and concern by serving as his own Minister of Education. In 1962 the Emperor facilitated the establishment of the university at Addis Ababa; he provided one of his palaces as the home for the new university, and the government assumed responsibility for a significant part of its budget. The rural health program based on the training of public health officers, sanitarians, and nurses at Gondar was launched in 1952. Ethiopian Airlines was established under a long-term contract with Trans-World Airlines and now provides services to major cities within the country as well as to an expanding number of countries in Africa, Asia, and Europe.

Because of the limited opportunities for advanced training at home, action was taken by the Ethiopian government to send a large number of young people abroad for undergraduate and graduate study. As a result, a total of not less than 500 and perhaps over 1,000 have received degrees in other countries; this is a significant minority of all undergraduate degree holders and includes all who have higher degrees.

A further step that has led to a considerable broadening and deepening of the nation's human resources was the highly successful effort of the Ethiopians to attract a substantial amount of foreign assistance from a great many different nations, much of it centered specifically on educational and training efforts. Alemaya College, now the Faculty of Agriculture of the university, which is heavily supported by USAID, was established and has been operated under contract by Oklahoma State University. Since its inception in the early 1950s it has trained 225 Ethiopians and a number of foreign students, all of whom have received Bachelor of Science degrees. The Swedish government has sponsored and underwritten the operation of a Building College in Addis Ababa which has educated and trained many building engineers, draftsmen, and skilled workers. Soviet Russia has recently assumed responsibility for the Technical Institute at Bahar Dar, which has an average enrollment of almost 250 students in each of its three-year programs; the graduates of this institute will represent an important addition to the small pool of craftsmen.

Several nations, including the United States, Israel, Germany, and the United Kingdom, currently provide substantial assistance in money and personnel to Haile Selassie I University. But significant foreign assistance involves more. Many critically important operations in the modern sector of the economy and society are managed and staffed by foreign experts, many of whom have spent a long time in the country and have contributed to the training and upgrading of their Ethiopian colleagues.

Another dimension of efforts to raise the level of skill and competence is the heavy reliance that the Ethiopian government has placed on sending people abroad for specialized courses. A great many opportunities for Ethiopians to study abroad have been made available by various nations as well as international bodies. Ethiopia has also had assistance from a considerable number of experts on the payrolls of international bodies, responsible for executing specific operational tasks, or recruited to provide general assistance to new government enterprises or activities.

While most of the efforts to facilitate the training of Ethiopian manpower have been made by foreign governments and international agencies, various voluntary groups have also contributed. They too have provided scholarships and financial support for educational efforts in Ethiopia and abroad as well as other forms of assistance.

Most of the efforts we have mentioned are related to the education and training of Ethiopians and to providing technical assistance to the Ethiopian government. Another facet of foreign assistance is related to the expansion of industry, commerce, and construction. While these sectors of the economy have expanded at only a modest rate, they have expanded, and many foreigners have come to live and work in Ethiopia under governmental or nongovernmental auspices, and have engaged directly and indirectly in the training of an Ethiopian staff. The Wonji Sugar Estates represent a large-scale effort of this kind. The many others include the shoe factory outside of Addis Ababa sponsored by the Czechoslovakian government, the several foreign oil companies operating in the country, and the oil refinery built at Assab on the Red Sea by the Soviets.

Another positive influence on training manpower in Ethiopia has been the establishment in Addis Ababa of the Organization for African Unity and the Economic Commission for Africa. These two major continental efforts have brought a large number of experts to Addis Ababa who contribute at least indirectly to broadening the horizons of many Ethiopians.

We can see that a great many events have occurred in Ethiopia since its liberation which have pointed the nation in new directions. The cutting edge of a modern sector has been sharpened. Addis Ababa has become an important center for the whole of Africa. The number of educated people in the country has increased substantially, and the foundations have been laid for a three-tier system of public education: primary, secondary, and collegiate. In addition, many specialized institutions have been established to provide trained manpower for teaching, telecommunications, the military, the highway system, and other advanced sectors. But all this progress—and it has been substantial, since our base is 1942— has been limited primarily to Addis Ababa and a few of the other cities and the countryside adjacent to these urban centers. Rural Ethiopia, which accounts for about 93 percent of the total population, has not yet been caught up significantly in this vortex of change.

At this point it may be helpful to introduce some basic data which will provide the reader with a frame within which to assess the analyses which are set forth in the following chapters.

The best available figures indicate that at the end of 1965 the population of Ethiopia was in the range of 22.2 to 22.6 million and the final results of the sample enumeration now underway is not likely to differ from this estimate by more than 1 million. From the field studies that have been completed, it appears that there has been a considerable population shift from the north to Shoa Province, which includes Addis Ababa.

The urban population—by which we mean those living in cities of 3,000 or more—approximates 1.5 million, or 6.7 percent of the total population. The two largest cities, Addis Ababa and Asmara, dominate the urban sector, and account for half of the total.

As in most developing nations, a high proportion of the total population is composed of children and adolescents. A third of the population (34 percent) is under 10 years of age and 45 percent is under 15. With about 5 percent older than 60, half of the population falls in the age range of 15 to 59.

In contrast to most developed nations, where women account for a slightly higher proportion of the total population than men, Ethiopia has about 400,000 (or roughly 2 percent) more males than females. Despite this slight overage of males in the population, there are somewhat more women (2 percent) than men in urban centers. An even more interesting finding is that in the smaller urban centers (excluding Addis Ababa and Asmara) there are very many more women than men in the prime age group of 20 to 29. In many towns there are twice as many women in this age group as men, which reflects the dearth of employment opportunities for men. In Addis Ababa, in contrast, there is a slight surplus of males in this age group.

The best estimate of literacy in the country as a whole places it in the 5 to 7 percent range. This estimate is liberal since it includes many who can read and write only a few words. As one might anticipate there are marked differences in literacy between the urban and rural population as well as between the sexes. Among those 10 years of age or older in the urban population, slightly over half of all males (52 percent) are literate. The corresponding figure for women is very much less—16 percent. On the basis of the population sampling that has been completed, rural literacy rates are estimated at 6.5 percent for men and .5 percent for women. In sum, between 10 and 13 percent of all men and between 1 and 1.5 percent of all women are literate.

A consideration of literacy by age indicates that for a long time a considerable proportion of urban males have long been literate. Even among men 65 years old or older, 29 percent are literate. The figure rises steadily among the younger age groups and is 65 percent for those in the group 10 to 14 years of age.

The rapid expansion of literacy among urban males has been exceeded by the gains of urban women in recent years. While literacy for urban women over 25 is well under 10 percent, it reaches 32 percent for the 15-to-19-year-old group and 44 percent for the 10-to-14-year-olds. The outstanding educational achievement of the last decade has been the large-scale entrance and retention of girls in the urban school system.

The rural picture is much less favorable. Literacy among rural women above the age of 25 is almost nil, and it has reached only 1.5 percent for the 10-to-14-year-olds. The data with respect to men are in some regards even more striking since they show a decline in recent years. Among the 20-to-44-year-old-group, 10 to 12 percent of the men are reported to be literate, while the figure declines to 7 percent among the 10-to-19-year-olds. A possible explanation for this unexpected trend might be the marked decline in church education in the countryside without a corresponding expansion of public educational opportunities. But the figures may overstate the facts. In terms of effective literacy there is little question that on balance the quality of education in government schools has been markedly superior to that provided by the ecclesiastical authorities.

With regard to the future, the only prospect for a substantial rise in general literacy hinges on the substantial expansion of the educational system in rural areas. No matter what additional gains are made in the urban areas, the literacy level for the population as a whole can rise above its present 5 to 7 percent level only through the successful penetration of education into the countryside.

In order to discuss the size and composition of the labor force in Ethiopia, we must decide on the key parameters. Anybody who travels in Ethiopia knows that it is common for young children—sometimes they are no more than 5 years old—to be entrusted with the task of watching the cattle. It would not be incorrect to include them in the labor force but we will not do so. A more difficult question involves adult women. The Planning Board tends to include most rural women in the labor force. We, however, have excluded most of them on the basis that they are engaged primarily in keeping house, rearing children, fetching water and firewood, and collecting dung. They occasionally help out at planting and harvesting time but for the most part agricultural work is done by male labor. It makes little difference whether rural women are included or excluded as long as one is consistent. By excluding most rural women, we calculate a labor force of just under 7 million on a base of 14.7 million in the appropriate age range, or 47.7 percent. The Planning Board figure is roughly 11 million. There are four major occupational groupings.

	Million	Percent
Agriculture	6.147	86.5
Industry, building, mining, laborers	.435	6.2
Services	.220	3.2
Sales, markets	.160	2.3

The remainder, less than 2 percent, is composed of a small number of professional and administrative workers, those engaged in communications, protective services, and a residual group.

There are no professional or skilled personnel in the rural areas. The only nonagricultural activities in rural areas are a very limited amount of selling and some services for households. It appears that the rural economy is an overwhelmingly self-sufficient one which the money economy has barely begun to penetrate.

In urban areas, workers in services and sales and laborers account in about equal proportions for the majority of the labor force. Professional, clerical, and communications employees together account for only slightly more than 11 percent of the urban labor force.

To round out these introductory data we will review the estimates of the size and growth of the economy and the components that account for the total output. The best data relate to the period 1961–63 inclusive and have been developed by both the Planning Board and the Central Statistical Office. While the figures of the Central Statistical Office are unofficial, they had the Planning Board's calculations to work from. For the year 1962, the beginning of the five year plan, Gross Domestic Product was estimated by the Central Statistical Office at E$110 per capita. The growth rate for the years 1962 and 1963 averaged about 3.5 percent per year, which appears to have been the approximate rate of growth of the economy in each of the two following years.

Table 1 sets out the composition of the Gross Domestic Product by industrial origin. The figures for 1963 show that agriculture accounted for just under two-thirds of total output (64.6 percent). Mining, manufacturing, and handicrafts together totaled 7 percent, followed by distribution, 6.6; public administration, 4.8; transportation and communications, 4.7; and housing, 4.1 percent. These five sectors account for 27 percent of the total output. The remainder is primarily in diversified services and construction.

It is worth pointing out that despite an estimated 2 percent growth in population, the annual growth of agricultural output did not exceed 1.5 percent between 1961 and 1963. At best, agriculture gives the impression of being stagnant; its output may in fact be declining slightly. Of the E$1,585 million of agricultural output in 1963, crops accounted for E$1,020 million. Coffee, a major export, accounted for E$125 million.

Governmental expenditures in 1963 totaled E$227 million, or just under 9 percent of Gross Domestic Product. Gross Domestic Capital Formation was just under E$300 million or about 12 percent of Gross Domestic Product.

As Table 2 indicates, in 1963 almost half of all capital formation took the form of improved land and buildings. The other important components in descending order were industrial machinery and equipment (E$32 mil-

TABLE 1

Gross Domestic Product by Industrial Origin at Factor Cost,
1961–63 (in E$ million)

	1961 [a]	1962 [b]	1962 [a]	1963 [a]	% Distribu... 1963
Total GDP	2,290.2	2,130.5	2,357.7	2,452.7	*100.0*
Agriculture and related industries	*1,545.0*	*1,480.6*	1,547.0	1,585.3	64.6
Agriculture	1,497.1	1,455.5	1,493.9	1,527.9	62.3
Forestry	41.8	23.3	46.7	50.4	2.0
Hunting	1.3	1.8 [c]	1.5	2.1	0.1
Fishing	4.8		4.9	4.9	0.2
Manufacturing and related industries	*146.9*	*113.3*	*162.4*	168.2	6.9
Manufacturing	45.2	34.9	57.3	61.0	2.5
Handicrafts and small industry	98.4	77.0	101.4	103.5	4.2
Mining and quarrying	3.3	1.4	3.7	3.7	0.2
Building and construction	40.4	44.5	44.9	45.3	1.8
Electricity	6.7	7.5	7.5	9.7	0.4
Distribution	138.8	136.1	149.3	162.0	6.6
Banking, insurance, and real estate	20.2	15.4	22.3	25.0	1.0
Transportation and communications	95.2	107.5	105.4	114.9	4.7
Public administration and defense, wages, and salaries	97.9	95.4	108.0	118.2	4.8
Ownership of dwellings	95.5	25.8	98.0	101.0	4.1
Education services, wages, and salaries	20.1	28.0	21.6	24.4	1.0
Medical and other health services	11.0	14.0	15.0	18.6	0.8
Domestic service	45.2	27.5	46.1	47.0	1.9
Other services	27.3	34.9	30.1	33.1	1.4

a Central Statistical Office estimates.
b Planning Board estimate. c Includes fishing.

lion), commercial road transport (E$23 million), and electrical machinery (E$12 million).

If attention is turned to the changes that occurred from 1961 through 1963, we find an increase of about 15 percent per annum in Gross Domestic Capital Formation with the most rapid growth in commercial road vehicles, industrial and electrical machinery, and telecommunications. Very little investment went into agriculture which, it will be recalled, accounted for almost two-thirds of the total annual output.

TABLE 2

Gross Domestic Fixed Capital Formation by Type
(in E$ million)

Type	1961	1962	1963
Total	228.7	275.0	296.2
Land and buildings	170.2	182.0	190.3
Residential buildings	109.4	97.5	104.3
Nonresidential buildings	15.5	15.4	17.0
Other commercial buildings and works	45.3	69.1	69.0
Vehicles, machinery, and equipment	58.5	93.0	105.9
Transport	22.4	57.7	41.3
Railroad equipment	—	1.3	2.3
Road, passenger	7.7	10.2	9.7
Road, commercial	11.3	13.4	22.7
Other transport equipment	3.4	32.8	6.6
Machinery and equipment	36.1	35.3	64.6
Agricultural	0.8	3.7	7.4
Mining and road construction	1.2	2.2	2.5
Industrial	23.0	16.7	31.7
Telephone, telegraph and radio	1.4	2.4	8.3
Electrical	6.9	7.4	12.0
Other	2.8	2.9	2.7

Another important dimension of the economic development of Ethiopia has been the growth of government revenues and expenditures during the past decade (Table 3).

TABLE 3

Revenues and Expenditures of the Ethiopian Government,
1957–58 to 1965–66 (in E$ million)

	REVENUES			EXPENDITURES			DEFICIT	
Year	Total	Ordi- nary	Extra- ordi- nary	Total	Ordi- nary	Extra- ordi- nary	Total	Ordi- nary
1957–58	168.0	140.4	27.6	175.5	146.1	29.4	−7.5	−5.7
1958–59	197.9	147.1	50.8	212.9	162.6	50.3	−15.0	−15.5
1959–60	150.3	133.1	17.2	157.6	136.9	20.7	−7.3	−3.8
1960–61	209.0	183.8	25.2	213.1	176.5	36.6	−4.1	+7.3
1961–62	252.8	199.4	53.4	253.1	190.2	62.9	−0.3	+9.2
1962–63	283.5	214.9	68.6	299.5	203.1	96.4	−16.0	+11.8
1963–64	359.7	272.1	87.6	359.0	297.6	61.4	+0.7	−25.5
1964–65	396.4	295.8	100.6	400.8	356.5	44.3	−4.4	−60.7
1965–66 [a]	457.0	393.2	63.8	485.4	385.1	100.3	−28.4	+8.1
1966–67 [b]	510.7	416.9	93.8	529.7	403.4	126.3	−19.0	+13.5

[a] Preliminary.
[b] Proposed.

Since the beginning of the 1960s, government revenues have tended to increase at the rate of 16 percent per annum compounded. Expenditures have kept pace. There has been a very substantial increase in extraordinary revenues and expenditures.

From a comprehensive analysis of the "Financing of the Unbalanced Budget in Ethiopia," by J. D. Van Pischke of the University's School of Business in the *Ethiopian Business Journal* of April, 1966, we can extract the following important findings. The budget for next year estimates that more than a third of the government's total expenditures will be financed with money obtained from the domestic banking system and from large amounts of funds given or loaned to Ethiopia from abroad—primarily from the latter source. The external debt of the Ethiopian government in July, 1965, for all loans and credits, committed and active, amounted to over E$427 million, of which E$266 million have been used. Of this sum, the United States accounted for E$121 million and the International Bank for Reconstruction and Development and the International Development Agency together accounted for E$89 million. The Eastern Bloc (the USSR, Czechoslovakia, and Yugoslavia) together accounted for E$44 million. Western Europe and Israel accounted for the remaining E$11 million.

About one-fifth of the ordinary expenditures of the Ethiopian government in the current fiscal year will be covered by E$74 million of foreign assistance. Most of the foreign assistance will be devoted to the ministries of National Defense, Interior, Education, and Public Health, and it will cover between one-quarter and one-third of the total expenditures of each ministry.

These few facts and figures should make clear the dependence of Ethiopia in its modernizing efforts on a continuing substantial level of foreign aid.

How can we summarize these developments? Ethiopia, with a population of approximately 22 million persons, is overwhelmingly agricultural with a very low per capita income and a very low rate of literacy. The economy is growing at a modest rate; in fact, it is growing slowly in light of the fact that more than half of its growth is absorbed by an increase in population. There is no basis in terms of present knowledge of the resources of the economy for postulating any spectacular increase in the rate of development. Even though the modest gains that have been made reflect in considerable measure the assistance received from abroad, gains in per capita income and in the terms of life will come only to the extent that the nation, aided and abetted by continuing help from abroad, learns how to make more effective use of its own resources, particularly its human resources.

It would be wrong to stipulate that Ethiopia is the prototype of developing nations either in sub-Sahara Africa or elsewhere. In some regards it is better off, since it largely escaped colonial domination and all of the ensuing political and psychological disturbances. In other regards it is more severely handicapped; it has one of the highest rates of illiteracy and one of the lowest levels of per capita income in the world.

Yet in the broader perspective of the economics of development, its problems are not very different from those faced by many African, Asian, and South American countries: a predominantly agricultural economy, an infrastructure inadequate for rapid industrialization, a low level of skill and competence, an unbridgeable gap between domestic savings and the capital requirements essential for accelerated development, the absence of any important natural resource. Its development, like the development of many other poor nations, hinges in the first instance on the enhanced productivity of its population, which is and will long remain in agriculture.

✦ 3 ✦

Strategic Manpower Issues

AS WITH all research, a manpower study will succeed
or fail depending on the questions which are posed. There
is a tendency among research workers to ask those questions that can be answered by the existing data. But if
the data determine the lines of analysis, it is likely that the
results may be irrelevant because they do not bear on important questions. This is particularly so in developing nations which are at an early stage of data collection.

On the other hand, is it worthwhile to pursue questions
which cannot be analyzed in depth because there are no
reliable data? The answer is simple: while statistics are
important they are not the only means of understanding
complex issues. In the absence of detailed statistical data
there are many ways in which pieces of information can be
combined to assess and illuminate specific manpower
issues. To illustrate with the matter of manpower shortages: without reliable data about the supply of trained
manpower and the flow into and out of the training
stream, and without information in depth about the
strength of the demand for trained manpower in various
sectors of the society, it is difficult to reach sound judg-

ments about the magnitude and severity of various manpower shortages.

But we need not be totally at sea. Wage and salary data
may provide a significant clue. The ease or difficulty with
which new graduates obtain employment is another. The
willingness of the Civil Service to permit certain departments to deviate from the established scales may be revealing. Pirating of personnel among employers can shed light
on the issue. So can the efforts employers make to train
technicians and skilled manpower to economize in the use
of scarce professional personnel. These are some of the
many scraps of information which if pieced together can
shed considerable light on this problem.

This chapter will seek to delineate some of the key
factors that determine the rate at which a nation is able to
develop its manpower resources and the effectiveness with
which it utilizes them. By focusing on a limited number of
issues we will seek to provide a framework within which a
more detailed analysis of Ethiopia's manpower problems
can be evaluated.

The first element is topographical. The ease with which
people can develop their competence and skills is very
much affected by where they have been born and live.
This is a matter of overriding importance in Ethiopia because its terrain makes it so difficult to bring services to the
countryside, especially to rural areas that lie any distance
from an arterial road. The importance of locale is reflected
in data which compare school attendance and literacy by
size of community.

With regard to school attendance, we found that in
1964–65, about 69 percent of all young people between
the ages of 7 and 14 living in urban centers were in school.
This was true of only 3.2 percent of rural children in the
same age group. The data on literacy provide an addi-

tional dimension since they emphasize that the larger the urban community, the higher the level of literacy. With regard to urban males 10 years of age and over, the literacy rate rises from an average of 46 percent in the small urban centers to 57 percent in the largest ones. Female literacy rates show the same tendency: it is 11 percent in the small cities and about 20 percent in the largest communities. Likewise, quality of education improves as we move from rural to urban areas, from small to large cities.

The explanations of such gross geographic differences are close at hand. The larger the community, the more attractive it is for trained people to settle and work there. The best teachers therefore tend to gravitate to the large centers. Second, the larger communities tend to have more economic resources and are therefore able to provide higher salaries and more amenities, which help them to attract and hold the better qualified members of the teaching profession.

What we have just said about educational penetration in different locations holds also for other important developmental efforts such as health and other basic services. Here too there is great difficulty in attracting trained personnel to live in the countryside, and, because of unsatisfactory roads, it is almost impossible to bring services to the outlying population. A recent map showing the location of all agricultural extension agents indicates that almost without exception they reside along the arterial highways. This means they were able to penetrate only short distances into the more isolated areas.

A second major axis is the relative importance of the private and governmental sectors as employers of trained manpower. In developed societies that are market-oriented, the private sector always accounts for more than half of the total economic activity, and frequently for three quarters or more. But this is not so in developing countries.

A few illustrations will help to indicate the overriding importance of the Ethiopian government as an employer of trained manpower. It has been calculated that not less than 95 percent of all college graduates—those educated in Ethiopia as well as those trained abroad—are currently employed in the governmental sector. Confirmation of this is found in a recent analysis of the large numbers who at one or another time studied and traveled abroad under programs sponsored by USAID. At the time of the survey, of a total of 875 recipients, only about 40 were working in the private sector.

Another indication of the predominant role of government is to review briefly the modern sectors of the Ethiopian economy and to assess the extent to which they have grown in response to either private or public investment. Education and health are overwhelmingly dependent on governmental funds, particularly since liberation. Church and nonprofit organizations still play a role in educational and health activities, but theirs has been a declining rather than an expanding one.

The largest proportion of governmental funds goes to the military. The most recently published data reveal that in 1965–66, the military spent about 27 percent of total budgeted ordinary expenditures. If we seek to identify the two most dynamic sectors of Ethiopia since liberation, education and the military stand out. No other sector has been transformed to the same extent.

The last two decades have seen a substantial effort to expand the road system. The Ethiopian government is currently seeking a further substantial highway loan from the World Bank. The highways are exclusively in the governmental domain.

The telecommunications network is constantly being expanded and improved. This too is a purely governmental enterprise. This is generally true of the generation and distribution of electric power. The railways and the Ethiopian Airlines are likewise quasi-governmental enterprises.

There is little point in continuing the roll. The Ethiopian government has been and continues to be the principal agent responsible for the establishment and expansion of the modern sector. Nor could it be otherwise. Ethiopia has at present no clear comparative advantages, whatever its potentials in coffee, meat production, grain output, and minerals may eventually turn out to be. Moreover, the local market is at present limited. While individual entrepreneurs may find it profitable to initiate or expand specific operations, any substantial growth of the private sector must wait upon the broadening and deepening of the infrastructure which alone can increase the opportunity for profit-making. For instance, one expert estimates that transportation cost per ton mile must be reduced by 80 percent if private enterprise is to expand significantly.

Several important manpower implications can be drawn from the above in addition to the proposition already advanced that government is the principal employer of trained manpower. Despite the sizable investments that have already been made in strengthening the nation's infrastructure, it is difficult to see how Ethiopia can progress unless additional large investments in infrastructure are made. Hence, the single most important determinant of the future demand for trained manpower will be the rate of growth in government expenditures.

Further, with government and quasi-governmental corporations employing most of the trained manpower, it is clear that the effectiveness with which the government organizes its operations and the efficiency with which it carries them out will largely determine the success of the country's modernization program. More specifically, the quality of political and professional leadership in the several government departments and agencies will have an overriding importance in determining how effectively the relatively large numbers of trained personnel are utilized. The efficiency of government holds the key to the progress of the economy and the society.

Another critical axis is the relation between the capacity of the educational and training system and the flow of students into and out of the system. Since liberation, Ethiopia has sought to advance on a great many different fronts, each of which required people with a wide variety of competences and skill, even though there were very few Ethiopians with the necessary knowledge and training. As noted earlier, the Emperor saw to it that many skilled Italians were encouraged to remain in the country rather than follow their defeated army homeward. Next, much of the trained manpower required for expansion was provided by foreign contractors, who, as in the case of highway and building construction, imported not only specialized equipment but also the talents and skills required to plan and execute their projects. Another variant was followed by the Wonji Sugar Estates, where from the start Dutch management has been in control. It has lately trained and promoted a considerable number of Ethiopians. However, the success of this, as well as several other large undertakings, was the direct result of foreign interests initially providing the managerial and technical manpower that was not available in Ethiopia.

Another important adaptation has been the considerable number of foreign experts who have come to Ethiopia and who have assisted their Ethiopian counterparts to broaden and deepen their skills.

But helpful as these expedients have been, they did not

provide as much competence and skill as the nation required. There has been a shortfall at almost every level. One important innovation which has helped to reduce the shortfall has been the rapid expansion of educational and training facilities in order to increase the supply of qualified people. But a developing country faces a dilemma when it proceeds along this route, and Ethiopia is no exception. Key to the expansion of the educational-training structure is an adequate supply of qualified instructors and trainees—in addition, of course, to adequate classrooms, equipment, dormitories, and financial resources for teachers' salaries and student stipends. While a forced expansion has taken place and much of the success in the nation's modernizing efforts can be ascribed to these efforts, it has not been possible in the past to establish and maintain a balance among the need for additional skills, training capacity, and competent trainees.

We have emphasized the pervasive shortages of professional and skilled personnel to meet the accelerated efforts of Ethiopia to modernize along a great many different fronts from the military to health. Small wonder that most manpower specialists have stressed the problem of current and prospective shortages of skill. But while these shortages are real and pressing and are likely to remain for a long time to come, this stress oversimplifies the problem. A consideration of shortages without a simultaneous consideration of utilization illuminates only part of the picture, sometimes the less important part.

We have noted selected facets of utilization: the great difficulties faced by the rural areas in attracting and holding trained people, and the critical role of government as the almost exclusive employer of college graduates and its importance in determining the effectiveness with which trained people are utilized.

Several additional dimensions of the supply-utilization

axis are worth exploring. The first relates to the difficulties in many developed, as well as developing, countries in finding the right balances between subprofessional and professional manpower. A vice-minister may spend a great portion of his time in activities that could better be left to his staff if they were competent. Many a graduate engineer must do simple drafting and elementary calculations because he has no technician at hand who could readily do simple tasks for him. This principle holds in many other fields. Determining the appropriate complementary requirements for different skill levels is an important task in manpower planning.

Another dimension of manpower utilization is the effectiveness with which organizations with large numbers of trained personnel are operated. Now, no organization, be it a government bureau, a school, a hospital, or a business concern, has only one goal—even the goal of utilizing its staff effectively. Of course, the proper use of staff is the obligation of every executive, but it is not the only challenge to which he must remain alert. An executive must be concerned with what his superior wants, and for various reasons his superior may be interested in a policy of inaction or very deliberate speed ahead rather than in making optimal use of his subordinates. Here the "underutilization" of trained manpower may reflect certain overriding organizational considerations. A school principal might be inclined to let his new teachers try out some of their new ways of instruction, but he is also concerned about the innate conservatism of the leadership in his community. As a consequence, he is likely to restrain his staff and place limitations on them which reduce their effectiveness.

When people find that they cannot make use of their talent and skills they are likely to respond in one of several ways. They may eventually stop trying and settle for drawing their salaries. Or they may decide "to play the game according to the rules," which means that they will be primarily concerned with self-aggrandizement. They will do their best to curry favor with their superiors. If this implies remaining idle and letting their skills tarnish, they will do so. What else can one expect of a man who has responsibilities and must look to the future?

In contrast, some cannot stand this type of self-emasculation and prefer to resign and take their chances elsewhere. They cannot settle for a waiting game full of frustration and inactivity. But it is important to note than when adverse conditions of employment lead to a high rate of turnover, such as is typical of the teaching profession in Ethiopia, they are likely to carry a considerable social cost. The individual who leaves may be better off, but the utilization of the teacher supply may be ineffective because of high turnover rates.

Another critical manpower axis in developing countries, and particularly in Ethiopia, is the relationship between trained foreigners and the local work force. Such a relationship must be dynamic. Implicit in a country's desire and intent to speed development is its recognition of its need to increase its own pool of skills. But a wide gap is likely to arise between desire and actuality. Skills which the local population does not have cannot be wished into existence. They must be developed, always at considerable cost of money and time. In the interim, the developing nation must use the skills of foreigners, individuals who may be long-term residents but who are not citizens, as well as others who are permitted or encouraged to enter the country specifically to lend a helping hand.

It is difficult to achieve a proper balance in this arena. Officials in developing countries tend to look askance at the requests of private and quasi-public enterprises to bring in specialists from the outside. They tend to over-estimate the competence of the local population. On the other hand, executives faced with an assortment of difficulties hope to ease their problems by attracting foreign experts on whom they know they can rely. Moreover, once the specialists are in the country, they are reluctant to let them go because they are likely to be much more experienced than their counterparts.

National manpower policy in developing countries must attempt to find the right stance with respect to such complex matters as who should be granted work permits, for how long, the conditions of renewal, the responsibility of foreign employers to train the local staff, the establishment of a schedule for the replacement of foreigners with nationals, the conditions governing the continuing in business of resident foreigners, and related matters.

One more issue must be placed in perspective. From many points of view, it is the most important since it cuts across all of the others. We refer to the overwhelmingly important matter of incentives and barriers to the effective development and utilization of manpower. Note was taken earlier of the distribution of educational and other developmental opportunities in urban versus rural areas. One important consequence of the demographic pattern prevailing in Ethiopia is the great hurdle that the rural population faces in developing its talent.

In addition to topography, law, administration, and market institutions also affect the development and utilization of the nation's manpower resources. For instance, in Ethiopia a premium is given to young people who have acquired a baccalaureate degree. The fact that they are paid a minimum salary of E\$450 per month—or more than double what the market pays to a high-school graduate—exerts a powerful pull in the direction of college. However, the best way into college is by earning the Ethiopian School Leaving Certificate (ESLC). And of the large numbers who sit for it, only a minority pass. Here is a major barrier to further study and a higher degree.

But it is not all bleak for those who fail. There are sub-professional and technical schools which offer the unsuccessful college applicant an opportunity to go on with his studies and acquire a skill. There are extension courses that provide a bridge to acquiring a diploma or in some cases to a second chance at a degree course.

One of the most interesting developments in the process of skill acquisition in Ethiopia are the considerable number of specialized schools from telecommunications to teacher training institutes that "tap off" young people at the tenth and eleventh grades and provide them with a subsidized educational experience. This is a powerful incentive.

Nor must the potency of the market be overlooked. When skills are scarce, as in the case of bilingual secretaries or skilled mechanics who can work on a wide range of machines, competition among employers will be reflected in strikingly high wage rates. These individuals are likely to earn the equivalent of or more than the salary earned by a doctor of philosophy or a government minister.

Most countries, and Ethiopia is no exception, make use of varying degrees of compulsion to influence the development and utilization of its manpower resources. Such a device is the year that all college students must spend in service outside of Addis Ababa. Similarly, the rule is that certain students must serve the government for two years for every year that they have been subsidized during their studies. Also officers of the armed forces must obtain the Emperor's permission for their release from service. All of these and other rules, regulations, and mechanisms influence in varying degrees who is educated and trained and the use which is made of the education and training which people acquire.

A manpower study must be cognizant of these several axes. If it is able to delineate the interrelationships among these several axes, it will be able to chart the directions for sound progress in developing the nation's manpower resources.

These key axes to which manpower planning and policies must be responsive in Ethiopia have their counterparts in other developing nations. The gap between the city and the countryside in terms of access to educational and other opportunities is characteristic of most developing nations which are agriculture-based. In fact, even the most advanced technological societies have not been able to do more than narrow the differentials between urban and rural communities; important discrepancies remain between the city dweller and the farmer in the opportunities available and possible earnings.

Likewise, there are differences in the treatment of the sexes. While girls and women in the urban centers of developing nations are slowly gaining access to schools and jobs from which they were previously barred, those who continue to live in the countryside are likely to be blocked from participating (surely participating equally) with boys and men in the new opportunities which open up. Where religion and tradition have narrowly circumscribed the role of women, as in Muslim countries and in countries with a strong Hispanic influence, the emancipation of women is likely to be much slower.

Despite the hopes and expectations of the United States and other Western countries that the private sector will play a prominent role in development, the pattern characteristic of Ethiopia differs little from the pattern of other economies in an early stage of transformation. The public and quasi-public sector dominates, and therefore the not-for-profit sector becomes the principal employer of trained manpower. Hence, it is the employment policies and practices of government which are a major determinant of manpower utilization.

This suggests another parallel. In Ethiopia, as in many other developing societies, a great deal of effort is directed to modernizing the military. Yet, in Ethiopia, as elsewhere, too little attention has been paid to the linkages that exist or can be established between the development and utilization of skills in the military and in the civilian sectors.

There are further parallels between the manpower problems that Ethiopia faces and those that confront many other developing nations. Every developing nation is attempting to find a balance between its educational and training institutions and the demands of the market for skills. However, at the level of collegiate and graduate education, serious imbalance has long plagued many countries in Southeast Asia and Latin America, as well as elsewhere, where graduates in the humanities are in gross oversupply, while severe shortages exist among scientific and engineering manpower.

The distortions go beyond the training people pursue and the skills the market requires, and include the incentive system and other potent forces that influence utilization of manpower. Almost every developing nation confronts the necessity of adjusting its wage structures to the objectives of its development plans; moreover, it must experiment to find the proper balance between relying on foreign nationals with special competences and providing opportunities for their own people to qualify for positions of responsibility.

The central manpower issues which engage Ethiopia are

not identical with those that engage its neighbors in East Africa, and they differ more from those of developing nations farther afield. But the differences do not vitiate the value for other countries of an analysis in depth of the Ethiopian situation. Many of the findings are directly relevant to the issues which many other developing nations face, and others, if appropriately applied, can prove helpful.

✦ 4 ✦

Transforming the Supply

NINETEENTH-CENTURY economists, particularly those trained in the tradition of the British classical school, agreed that the best way for a nation, including an under-developed nation, to progress was to specialize in the production of commodities for which it had some special advantage. This carried with it the implication that a non-industrialized area could make the fastest progress by growing crops or mining resources which industrialized nations desired and which they sought to acquire through trade. But as time went on it became less clear to the developing nations whether in fact specialization would result in significant gains in their standard of living. After all, the rapid gains made in wealth and welfare by the technologically advanced countries appeared to rest on their successful industrialization. As a result, the developing nations looked in the same direction—they too sought to industrialize.

Once they decided to industrialize, their primary efforts were devoted to obtaining large amounts of capital through investments, loans, or grants. For clearly industrialization required large capital inputs. But it was not long before the developing nations came to understand that capital alone was not sufficient. The speed of their economic advance appeared to depend also on their educating and training a corps of competent managers, administrators, professionals, technicians, and skilled workers. Only the availability of a pool of capable people could turn inert capital into a productive resource.

The last decade has witnessed an increasing concern in developing countries with the development of their human resources as a precondition and accompaniment to modernization and industrialization. Accordingly they have centered their attention on broadening and deepening their educational system from primary school to the university, as they have understood that the formal educational system provides the base for the acquisition of specialized competences and skills.

In recent years development experts have had some second thoughts about the approach. They have begun to consider elements previously ignored, such as the costs involved in rapidly expanding an educational system; the priorities that must be set among the different levels and types of education; the ability of the economy and the society to absorb the numbers who are educated and trained; the potentialities of using noninstitutional forms of training for certain types of skill acquisition; and the necessity to keep a balance in the expansion process between financial resources, the training of teachers, the flow of qualified pupils, and the availability of other resources such as school buildings and equipment. These are just a few of the complex considerations that have come to the fore recently to moderate the blanket enthusiasm of the protagonists of the view that education holds the key to development.

Against this background we must seek to sort out the structure and functioning of the educational and training system in Ethiopia in order to assess the numbers of educated and trained persons that are currently being turned out and that are likely to be turned out in the years immediately ahead. Once the capacity and capabilities of the educational–training structure have been critically evaluated, the other variables in the equation—the demand for trained manpower and their utilization—will be reviewed. When these three elements have been appraised, the directions for manpower policy will be easier to chart.

The analysis will begin with a consideration of the scale of the different parts of the formal educational structure and the expansion that has been taking place in recent years. Particular attention will be paid to the size and nature of the pupil flow through successively higher levels of the system. This will be followed by a consideration of the ways in which pupils are tapped off for various types of specialized education and training programs at the tenth grade or succeeding years. The problems of the university will be reviewed. Special attention will be directed to the critical area of teacher supply and retention. Finally the incentive structure—and disincentives such as bonding—will be critically assessed. Once these stages in the analysis have been completed, we should be able to reach reasonable agreement about the probable transformation of the manpower supply in Ethiopia in the years immediately ahead.

A good way to begin the assessment of the educational system is to estimate the numbers who have been enrolled in school since 1950, when the government initiated its effort to expand its educational system. Although Table 4 is a crude estimate, it can be used as a start. Allowance has

been made for students repeating one or more grades, and
the totals are net.

TABLE 4

*Total Number of Students Attaining Selected Grades,
1950 through 1965*

Grade	Number of Students
1	800,000
2	600,000
4	200,000
8	75,000
10	25,000
12	6,500
College: 1 year	4,500
College graduate	1,000

Several important findings can be deduced. The absolute number of children and young people enrolled in
school has been expanding rapidly, especially since only a
few attended in the early 1950s. The attrition between the
first grade and the fourth grade (literacy level) has been
very substantial—perhaps 60 percent. The base from which
professional, technical, and skilled manpower is largely
drawn—tenth grade—is only 25,000. A high proportion of
young people who succeed in completing high school also
succeed in entering college, but attrition in college is very
high, partly due to the large number who leave with a certificate or diploma after two years. The expansion of the
educational system is indicated by a closer consideration of
events during the past five years by comparing enrollments
in 1959–60 with those in 1964–65. The following sets out
the percentage of the appropriate age group enrolled in
each grade. (Although many students are over-age in
grade, this does not significantly affect the validity of the
comparisons) .

AGE	GRADE	PERCENTAGE OF AGE GROUP ENROLLED	
		1959–60	*1964–65*
7	1	14.9	17.8
10	4	5.1	6.3
12	6	2.5	3.8
14	8	1.8	2.3
16	10	.6	1.1
18	12	.2	.3
19	College: 1 year	.1	.2

It is important to bear in mind when reviewing the above that the population was expanding rapidly during these five years so that the modest percentage improvement masks a more substantial increase in the total numbers enrolled. In point of fact the rate of increase in enrollment for all grades amounted to 12 percent per annum compounded. The following sets out the growth in enrollments during this five-year period at different levels of the educational system:

Grades	Five-Year Growth (in percent)
1–4	71
5–6	89
7–8	70
9–12	151
Total: 1–12	77

The relatively high expansion in grades nine to twelve must be interpreted also against the relatively heavy but steady tap-offs for specialized programs that occur in the tenth grade and which will be discussed below. The expansion of the educational system can also be seen by reviewing the absolute figures of students enrolled five years ago and last year.

Grades	1959–60	1964–65
1–4	174,400	301,200
5–6	24,700	46,500
7–8	14,600	24,700
9–12	6,200	15,600
Total: 1–12	219,900	388,000
College	827	1,643

Between 1959–60 and 1964–65 total enrollment in grades one through twelve increased from almost 220,000 to 388,000. So much for the recent past. What of the near future? We have projected the recent trend and estimate that during the next four years enrollment in these twelve grades will be as follows:

1965–66	427,000
1966–67	467,000
1967–68	509,000
1968–69	547,000

If the last figure is reached or approximated, it will mean that during the decade of the 1960s the total educational system of Ethiopia will have expanded one and a half times.

An even more revealing analysis is to compare the expansion at different levels. For this purpose we will compare the base year 1959–60 with the estimated enrollment in 1968–69:

Grades	1959–60	1968–69
1–4	175,000	389,000
5–6	25,000	79,000
7–8	15,000	46,000
9–12	6,000	34,000

These figures indicate that, if our estimates for 1968–69 prove correct, there will be a relatively more rapid increase in the higher than in the lower levels of the system. The base from which professional and trained manpower is drawn will expand almost sixfold while enrollments in the early grades will slightly more than double.

How sound are our projections? It is hard to say. But we were unable to delineate any visible forces that are likely to alter significantly the historical trend towards expanding enrollments. Nevertheless, it is important to note that the estimates prepared in connection with the large educational loan that the Ethiopian government recently negotiated with the International Development Association to expand its secondary schools differ in several major respects from our estimates.

The IDA planning figures anticipate a growth in the next few years of 75 percent for all grades, one through twelve, in comparison to our much lower estimate of 41 percent. Despite our lower overall estimate we anticipate considerably higher enrollments in the seventh through the twelfth grades than does the IDA plan. The difference can be explained by the fact that the IDA estimates were constructed with an eye to a controlled expansion of junior and senior high schools while ours reflect the strong pressures for expansion that will be exerted by the larger number of students who will have completed the earlier grades successfully.

We do not believe that the government will be able to deny a growing percentage of sixth graders the opportunity to move ahead. The attrition is high enough without the government's deliberately seeking to increase it. In addition, we do not understand why the IDA estimates allow for only 25 percent attrition between the first and second grades when the most recent data show an attrition rate of just less than 50 percent.

In any case both estimates agree that Ethiopia will continue to experience a steady expansion in its educational system. The following compares the proportion of the school-age population enrolled in varying grades for the beginning and the end of the decade.

PERCENTAGE ENROLLED

AGE	GRADE	1959–60 (actual)	1968–69 (historical projections)	1968–69 (IDA estimates)
7	1	14.9	22.5	25.5
10	4	5.1	7.6	10.9
12	6	2.5	5.1	5.5
14	8	1.8	3.4	3.2
16	10	.6	1.9	1.6
18	12	.2	.6	.7

This reaffirms the point made earlier: the relative expansion will be considerably more rapid in the upper grades.

We must now take a closer look at the size of the pool out of which most of the nation's professional and skilled manpower is obtained. In 1964–65, the following numbers of young people were still in the main educational stream.

Grade	Number of Students
10	4,300
11	2,500
12	1,300
College: 1 year	844
2 years	464
3 years	169
4 to 5 years	166

On the face of it, these are modest figures which become even more modest when additional information is introduced about the proportion of those in the twelfth grade who successfully pass the examination for the ESLC. Slightly under 90 percent of all twelfth graders sit for the examination but only about 25 percent pass. While there has been much discussion of late about the suitability of the examination both for assessing the general competence of high-school seniors as well as their capacity to cope successfully with college studies, it is probably premature to do away with the examination, especially before a more adequate instrument has been designed and validated.

The fact that a high percentage of college entrants fail to complete their studies satisfactorily cannot be ignored when discussing the future of the ESLC. The opponents of the ESLC argue that those admitted to the university who have not passed the examination do no worse in their college studies, and possibly even a little better, than those who have passed. They believe, therefore, that the examination is not valid as a screening instrument. But until the data are collected and analyzed more carefully, and consideration given to the courses of specialization followed by the group of passing students and the courses pursued by the failing students, the examination should be retained as a screening mechanism by the university. There are good reasons, however, to supplement it with another which could attest to the fact that a student has satisfactorily completed the twelfth grade whether or not he has the qualifications for college entrance. There is no need to use a single instrument for both purposes—graduation from high school and college entrance.

The following sets forth our best estimates of the future growth of the student population in high school through this decade.

It should be recalled that the IDA estimates are considerably lower than those set out above. We estimate that in 1968–69, just over 34,000 students will be in high school while IDA assumes a total of just over 27,000. However, the important point is that there will be, in percentage terms, substantial increases in the upper grades of high school, but the absolute numbers will still be small.

High-School Enrollment

GRADE	ACTUAL		ESTIMATED		
	1964–65	*1965–66*	*1966–67*	*1967–68*	*1968–69*
9	7,540	8,800	10,920	12,180	14,630
10	4,300	6,030	7,040	8,740	9,740
11	2,520	3,100	4,340	5,070	6,290
12	1,270	1,680	2,060	2,890	3,390

Let us consider the adequacy of the student flow through the high-school system by reviewing the alternatives that young people face when they have entered the tenth grade. These young people have a long, hard struggle to reach the tenth grade, and only a minority drop out at this point or in the eleventh or twelfth grades. But some will drop out either because of lack of interest or capacity to cope with the work, or because of economic and other pressures. Another group will go to the twelfth grade with the hope and expectation of entering college but, as we noted earlier, many of them will fail the ESLC. Of these students many will eventually get into college through programs that do not demand the ESLC, or after they obtain some additional qualifications. Some, however, will terminate their formal education at this point. Another group will proceed "normally," that is, they will pass the ESLC and go on to the university. The fourth group will be tapped off during the last two years of high school to enter a program in one of the considerable number of specialized training institutions that Ethiopia has developed over the past decade.

These training institutions can be distinguished by their

field of specialization: primarily they cover education, health, and technical areas. This list is constantly changing. Some years ago, the Ministry of Mines ran a school. Recently the Ministry of Agriculture established a new institution, the School for Animal Health. For the most part students are tapped off in the tenth or eleventh grade for these schools although the new School for Animal Health selects candidates from the twelfth grade and from among high-school graduates.

TABLE 5

Drop-Outs and Tap-Offs from Secondary Schools,
1962–63 to 1965–66

	1962–63	1963–64	1965–66
Total Students: Grades 9–11	8,628	10,931	14,363
Total drop-outs	2,097	2,822	3,553 [a]
Tap-Offs	1,229	1,545	2,107
Net drop-outs	868	1,277	1,446
Students remaining	6,531	8,109	10,810
Total drop-out rate	24%	26%	25%
Tap-Off rate	14%	14%	15%
Net drop-out rate	10%	12%	10%

[a] Estimated.

Table 5 sets forth the statistics of tap-offs in relation to total secondary school enrollments and drop-outs. Several findings can be deduced. The tap-off rate has been about 15 percent for each of the last three years. In absolute numbers it has almost doubled. The true drop-out rate cannot be estimated because some of the youngsters who leave school and who do not enter one of the specialized training institutions may in fact continue their training in less formal environments, such as the programs operated by the Highway Authority, Ethiopian Airlines, and certain large private employers that combine a job offer with the

opportunity for on-the-job training and even some classroom instruction. Presumably, a young man who continues in school until the tenth grade has something to offer
somebody, even if he does not have the qualifications for
entrance into one of the preferred programs.

TABLE 6

Tap-Offs by Type of Institution Entered, 1963–1965

	1963	*1964*	*1965*
Total	*1,229*	*1,545*	2,087
Education			
Primary (teacher training institutes)	476	810	1,070
Laboratory School	158	166	263
Health			
Nursing	70	72	79
Malaria control	30	34	43
Laboratory technician	9	—	10
Pasteur Institute	—	—	10
Public Health School	59	71	89
Technical Institutes			
Telecommunications	35	40	91
Bahar Dar Institute	230	180	250
Commercial School	30	30	30
Other			
Awasa Community Development	60	70	80
Air Force Academy	72	72	72

Table 6 sets forth the distribution of tap-offs by school
during the past three years. It indicates the very large part
played by the teacher training institutes which, together
with the Laboratory School, account for considerably more
than half of all the tap-offs in 1965.

To round out the picture of secondary vocational education, reference must be made to the long-established agricultural high school in Jimma and a smaller one in Ambo
and to the two relatively large vocational schools at Addis

Ababa and Asmara. The latter two had a combined enrollment of over 800 in 1965–66. Two others—the Commercial
School at Addis Ababa and the Bahar Dar Institute are included in the table dealing with tap-offs.

Current projections under the IDA plan set the tap-off
figure for 1967–68 at 2,700, an increase of roughly 30 percent in three years. But if the army, in its efforts to reduce
its shortages of officers, moves in the direction of tap-offs to
increase enrollments in its academy, and if other government agencies find that it would be desirable to increase
the number of graduates from their specialized schools, the
above modest projection may prove to be low. We believe
that this is likely to be the case, and we have projected
total secondary enrollments on the basis of the historical
trend rather than the more modest IDA figures.

It should be noted that the IDA Plan, despite its overall
conservatism, contemplates a rapid increase in the enrollment of the vocational high schools in Addis Ababa and
Asmara—from 623 in 1965–66 to 1,335 in 1968–69 in
Addis Ababa and from 231 to 729 in Asmara.

Several points should be noted about the tap-off system.
Many young people, especially from the rural areas and
from small towns, are too impoverished to continue their
education on their own after they have completed the
ninth or tenth grade. Their families are unable to help
them. Their only chance to stay in school and to acquire a
skill is through entrance into a subsidized program where
they will be assured of tuition, maintenance, and pocket
money. This, the specialized schools are able to provide for
those whom they select.

Because of the intense competition for admission to
these specialized schools, especially the best of them, the
group that is finally selected contains some youngsters with
excellent potential. Many of these young people, were

their families to support them, would be able to finish secondary school and enter the university without trouble. But they could not survive another two years on their own. Many who undertake teacher training, instruction in telecommunications, or who join the air force are more concerned with keeping themselves upwardly mobile than they are interested in the particular occupation for which

TABLE 7

Enrollment[a] in Haile Selassie I University by Faculty, 1961–62 to 1965–66

	1961–62	1962–63	1963–64	1964–65	1965–66	% Distribution 1965–66
Total	*948*	*1,041*	*1,601*	*1,639*	*2,056*	*100.0*
Arts	338	287	299	269	332	16.1
Agriculture	204	221	221	141	211	10.3
Education		129	210	414	584	28.4
Business			148	190	277	13.5
Science	94	78	122	134	122	5.9
Engineering	147	135	203	187	188	9.1
Building College	110	102	111	105	60	2.9
Law			20	68	94	4.6
Medicine			5	17 [b]	19	0.9
Public Health	45	58	75	76	104	5.1
Pharmacy			16		20	1.0
Social Work		16	26	22	26	1.3
Theology	10	15	19	16	19	0.9
General Studies			126			

[a] Includes diploma programs.
[b] Medicine and Pharmacy combined.

they are training. This presages considerable occupational shifting at a later time.

The substantial numbers of young people who enter vocational school or get tapped-off for one of the specialized training institutions, when added to the minority who, for sundry reasons, drop out along the way, are one reason that the university faces a problem in securing a qualified student body.

To set the stage for the discussion of student flow through the university, we will set out the growth of the institution since its founding in 1961–62 through the amalgamation of a group of independent colleges. Table 7 presents the basic data on enrollments by faculty for the first five years of the university's existence. It should be noted that included in these totals are students pursuing a two-year course of studies for which they receive a diploma, not a degree.

Several points are worth noting. Arts and Agriculture failed to grow over the quinquennium; the newly established faculties of Education and Business together currently account for more than 2 out of every 5 students. Science and Engineering together account for only about 1 in 6 students. The table does not indicate that a decision has been made to shift the Building College out of the university structure.

Table 8 shows enrollment over the quinquennium by year of study. These data indicate that while total enrollment more than doubled, the numbers reaching the junior and senior years showed much more modest gains. Only a part of this difference can be explained by the time required for an increased inflow to be reflected in the higher grades.

The university loses a great many students after they begin their studies. Data for 1964–65 for selected faculties show that while Agriculture has a high retention rate during the four-year course—in the 80 percent range—the average for the university as a whole, excluding Education, shows a loss of about one-third between the first and second years, and a comparable loss between the second and third years. Hence only slightly more than 2 out of 5 students reach their senior year. The retention rate for Science is low (1 out of 3) and for Engineering very low (1 out of 8).

TABLE 8

University Enrollment by Grade, 1961–62 to 1965–66

	1961–62	*1962–63*	*1963–64*	*1964–65*	*1965–66*
Total	*938*	*1,252*	*1,444*	*1,516*	*1,945*
I	300	481	740	797	945
II	266	265	268	429	516
III	202	272	223	168	274
IV/V	170	234	213	122	210

What is in store for the university? Currently 42 percent of those whom it admits hold an ESLC; the majority are admitted under special criteria. For instance, in 1964–65, 407 passed the examination (or its equivalent) and the university admitted 797. The comparable figures for 1965–66 were 519 and 945. We anticipate that the number who pass the examination will increase over the next quinquennium from 519 to 1,317.

Such a substantial increase will present the university with several options. It can take advantage of it to improve the quality of the students whom it admits by opening the spigot only slightly. Its other option will be to admit a somewhat larger number; if it increases its enrollment rapidly there will be little or no increase in quality as reflected in the proportion of those with an ESLC among its entrance class. If it admits only 100 more students during each of the following three years, the proportion of the entrance class with the ESLC will rise to about 3 out of 4; with an admission policy of 150 new students annually the rate would be 2 out of 3. And if 300 were added yearly, the rate would not be much different from what it is at present since it would still be slightly less than 1 out of 2.

There is general agreement among those who have considered the matter—the administration, the faculty, and the Chancellor's Advisory Committee—that the present attrition rate is distressingly high and that special efforts must be made to reduce it if the university's resources and the nation's manpower is not to be wasted. Some reduction in attrition can undoubtedly be achieved by special efforts to remedy some weaknesses in student preparation in the summer before they begin their studies and by additional efforts during their freshman year. A clearly desirable approach would be to strengthen the level of instruction in secondary schools, but it is unlikely that this will prove practical in the years immediately ahead when, as will be demonstrated later, competent teachers will continue in very short supply.

The decision as to the size of the first-year class must be made with reference to a great number of determinants, including in particular the capability of the university to handle a larger number of pupils with its present staff and facilities and the national need to expand the supply of certain types of trained manpower. But weighty as these and other considerations are, the authorities must recognize that in the face of the very high attrition which the university has been experiencing, there is a strong presumption in favor of its restricting its intake in the next few years. It is doubtful whether it can significantly reduce the serious wastage reflected in its high drop-out rate unless it improves the quality of its entering student body.

Crucial to a discussion of the educational-training structure and its potentialities for expansion is the outlook for teaching personnel at all levels of the educational system.

The number of eligible students is one major determinant of the ability of the system to expand; the other critical factor is the availability of teachers.

This is an overview of how matters now stand. Prior to the post-World War II expansion of education, responsibility for instruction in Ethiopia was divided between the clergy and foreigners. The few good schools, for the most part in Addis Ababa, were under the direction of foreigners and the staff was composed of foreigners.

As one might have anticipated, those with a modest amount of education frequently were instructing youngsters who had less or none. In the early days of the expansion, the level of teacher preparation was very low indeed. During the years, however, there has been pronounced improvement in the quality of teacher preparation, deficient as it may still appear to be against the standards of the Ministry of Education.

Table 9 sets forth the changes which have taken place in the level of preparation of elementary school teachers over the past twelve years. In 1953–54, 9 out of 10 teachers had six grades of education or less! In the last year for which data are available (1964–65), the proportion was little more that 1 out of 5—still a high proportion but a tremendous improvement over the base year. A similar finding emerges when one considers the number of elementary school teachers who have attended high school or gone beyond. Here the figures are equally startling—in twelve years the proportion increased from 2 percent to 45 percent of the total!

The problem of teacher preparation is more acute in the higher grades—that is, in grades seven to twelve where students must be instructed in English and where they must master more complicated subjects such as mathematics and science. One source of teachers for junior high school has been the teacher training institutes, although most of their graduates have taught in the lower grades. In the decade 1952 to 1961 inclusive the four teaching training institutes graduated a total of about 2,800 teachers. An almost equal number were graduated in the four years 1962–63 through 1965–66. The annual number of graduates during the next several years is estimated at about 800 and thereafter the level is expected to rise to 1,300. We will not enter at this point into a discussion of teacher turnover; it is nevertheless clear that these teacher training institutes have played a large and expanding role in the preparation of primary and junior high-school staffs and have been responsible in considerable measure for the improvement in the quality of teacher preparation.

TABLE 9

Years of Education Achieved by Elementary School Teachers, 1953–54 and 1964–65

	1953–54		1964–65	
	Number	*Percent*	*Number*	*Percent*
Total	*2,013*	*100*	*6,639*	*100*
9	45	2	*2,973*	45
7–8	160	8	2,186	33
1–6	*1,808*	90	*1,480*	22
6	448			
4–5	512			
less than 4	848			

What about high-school teachers? Here Ethiopia has improvised. The government initially staffed its high schools primarily with Indian contract teachers. Recently, the expansion of secondary schooling has been predicated on the utilization of large numbers of Peace Corps volunteers. Ethiopian teachers represent a minority group. In 1963–64 there were 1,055 teachers in secondary schools. Of this number 400 were Ethiopians; Peace Corps volunteers accounted for slightly more than half of the 655 foreign teachers. It should be observed in passing that the number of Ethiopians teaching in high school who have obtained their baccalaureate degrees apparently number no more than 10!

Several years ago in response to the present and prospective shortages on the teaching front, the university undertook to establish a School of Education with the aim of training high-school teachers and administrators for the entire government system. When the school experienced great difficulties in recruiting adequate numbers of applicants, it moved to establish a special feeder institution in the form of the Laboratory School, which admitted young people in the eleventh grade and steered them in the direction of the Faculty of Education. Including the year of Ethiopian University Service, which students must perform in their junior year, there is a six-year period between admission to the Laboratory School and graduation from the university. While there are currently over 600 students in the School of Education there is only a very small number (6 in total) in the two upper classes. Therefore, there will be no significant number of graduates in Education until the end of the decade when, it is anticipated, the annual number of graduates may approximate 80 to 100.

In addition to its degree program, the university has instituted a two-year diploma program. While here too the number of graduates is still very small—around 20 per year—it is scheduled to increase fairly rapidly to around 70 or 80 by the end of the decade.

The problem of teacher supply, considered solely from the vantage point of training institutions within the country and additions from overseas, reveals the following stark points. There will be a continuing and large shortfall in the number of qualified Ethiopian teachers for junior and senior high schools. This fact helps to explain the very low estimates of the inflow of new students at the seventh and ninth grade that underlie the IDA plans. But we seriously question whether the authorities will be able to withstand the pressure for admission. In fact they have already begun to plan for an expansion beyond the IDA program. This past year the principal of one large urban secondary school was ordered to find room for an additional several hundred pupils!

With regard to foreign teachers, the Ethiopian government is currently actively recruiting in India. After a period of uncertainty, it has also requested the U.S. government to increase the number of Peace Corps volunteers who can be assigned to high-school teaching. Those so assigned currently number just under 500.

A comprehensive analysis of the supply of secondary school teachers would have to assess also the availability of instructors for vocational and technical curricula. Suffice it to say in this connection that the shortages of competent instructors are acute and are likely to remain so, despite the efforts of the United States to assist in the training of vocational teachers for the comprehensive high schools which are now being planned. We must also include in any discussion of teacher supply the staffing needs of the specialized schools that fall outside, but run parallel to, the main educational system.

We can summarize this analysis of manpower supply in Ethiopia along the following lines. There has been, and there is every indication that there will continue to be, a steady if unspectacular increase in the educational and training system at every level—from the first grade of elementary school through the fourth and fifth year of college. The increases in enrollments and in the number of graduates which have already taken place and which will continue to take place are likely to permit the staffing of the first six grades by teachers who will be better prepared than their predecessors. This in turn suggests that, with an expanding system of basic education (grades one to six) and with an improvement in the quality of the teaching staff, the numbers knocking on the doors of junior and senior high school will increase substantially.

A major manpower difficulty will be the training of an adequate number of qualified teachers for the grades seven to twelve. There is little or no prospect that the present training structure is adequate to the task—a subject that we will explore more fully later. For better or worse, Ethiopia will long remain dependent on foreigners to staff a considerable proportion of its secondary schools. The situation with regard to competent vocational instructors is so difficult that great caution should be exercised in all plans that carry with them an increased requirement for such staff.

With regard to the flow of students qualified to pursue college work, we have seen that the university faces a simple choice: if it wants to reduce its exceedingly high attrition, its total enrollment must be kept under tight control and permitted to expand only modestly. For the university has faced and will undoubtedly continue to face severe competition from the specialized schools that tap off large numbers of the better qualified tenth graders.

This concludes our introduction to the education-training problems of Ethiopia. Later chapters carry the analysis further.

To what extent have we delineated basic educational issues which have pertinency and applicability to the problems of other developing nations? We have noted that Ethiopia has an excessively high rate of illiteracy, a reflection primarily of its predominant rurality and impenetrable terrain. But apart from such unique characteristics many developing nations face educational challenges much like those that have just been identified.

For instance, the pressure to expand education—at every level—is characteristic of every developing nation. The fact that many economists now warn about the potential waste of resources which might result from overinvesting in education has not mitigated the forces operating to expand the demand for schooling. Nor have their warnings provided politicians with the armor they need to withstand the mounting pressure.

The fact that major international agencies concerned with development have now entered the financing of education, as in Ethiopia, indicates that under certain circumstances large-scale expenditures for education are considered a desirable objective of capital investment. But any country, developing or developed, must exercise caution about the scale and scope of its educational expenditures— for these expenditures can quickly preempt a significant part of the budget and the returns are likely to be long delayed.

The appropriateness of a nation's educational structure is easy to assume but hard to prove. In many developing countries the educational endeavor, especially at the secondary and collegiate levels, is often a pale imitation of a European structure which may reveal deficiencies even in the country of origin. But once established, an educational system cannot be easily changed, and so its deficiencies are likely to take a large and continuing toll. Not much is gained, and sometimes considerable is lost, when a developing nation becomes aware that its imitative structure has limitations and moves to remodel along different lines. Frequently it is unable to free itself completely from its past and at the same time it cannot take full advantage of the new; and so it remains suspended between two quite different systems, unable to exploit the strengths of either.

Many former colonial territories, now independent nations, have followed for too long a system of education patterned after London or Paris. But it does not follow that these new nations are better off when they respond enthusiastically or under pressure to American advisers who seek to graft on to their structures an imitation of our landgrant college or vocational high school. The transformation must be much more carefully planned and implemented. No foreign model is likely to fit, and grafting requires great skill.

To illustrate: it may be that the examinations used to screen applicants for British universities are ill suited to the needs of many former British colonies and other nations which have had tie-ins with the University of London. But it does not follow that the American system, in which high-school graduation provides entrance to the state university, is a preferred approach. Most universities in the developing nations show appallingly high attrition rates even in the face of rigid screening devices. We can say therefore that there may be no gains and possibly serious losses entailed in a precipitate shift away from external examinations.

Similarly, since most developing nations are sorely in need of more skilled workers and technicians, adjustments in the educational system which might contribute to this end would be generally beneficial. But this does not mean that the developing nations should be encouraged to develop vocational high schools or polytechnical institutions along American or Russian lines without assurance that they can secure the teaching staffs required and absorb the high costs. There may be better ways for them to meet this problem.

In fact one of the costly errors that characterizes the educational planning of most developing nations is their preoccupation with the formal educational system for the development of skills to the neglect of the potential inherent in other approaches, particularly those related to formal and informal training within various enterprises, military and civilian alike.

The process of skill acquisition, even in advanced societies, has not been adequately delineated, and the relationships between the world of school and the world of work are far from smooth. It is not surprising that educators in most developing nations have moved ahead on their own, neglecting to dovetail their plans with the training efforts and particularly the training potential of enterprise.

No developing nation seeking to broaden and deepen its educational and training structure is likely to encounter exactly the same problems as those which have confronted and are confronting Ethiopia. But the Ethiopian experience should reveal the key constraints on the expansion of education and the key relationships between the education and the economy.

✦5✦

The Structure of Demand

MANPOWER specialists contend that developing economies require a large number of professional and skilled
manpower; these countries have relatively few educated
and trained people and if more were available they could
be readily absorbed. This chapter will review the growth,
present structure, and the shape of the Ethiopian economy
that is likely to develop in the near future in order to get
a better idea of the nature of its future demand for trained
manpower.

This is what we know about the recent growth of the
economy. As indicated earlier, the increases in GNP have
been of the order of 3½ percent per annum. With population increasing at about 2 percent, the per capita increase
in GNP has been about 1½ percent. This is a modest rate
of expansion.

We have noted that the dominant agricultural sector
is expanding at such a slow rate that it may not even be
keeping pace with the growth in population. Therefore we
must look particularly at what has been happening in the
nonagricultural sector.

In 1962, the Five Year Plan for Economic Development

estimated employment in the nonagricultural sector as follows:

Agriculture (industrial)	1,300
Mining	4,550
Clerical	1,800
Manufacturing	27,600
Handicrafts	186,000
Construction	62,800
Transportation	18,180
Communications	2,200
Trade	28,500
Catering	7,600
Financial	1,200
Education	44,580
Public Health	9,200
Community Development	220
Government administration	19,200
Other services	4,850
	419,800

How can we interpret this structure? Handicrafts is primarily the manufacture and tailoring of cloth for *shamas,* the national garb of Ethiopia. These two groups of workers account for approximately 80 percent of the total. The other significant groups are those engaged in grain milling, coffee and grain cleaning, and shoemaking. From scattered data there is a suggestion that employment in handicrafts may be growing at the rate of 5 percent per annum.

The next largest industry in terms of employment is construction, which is overwhelmingly concentrated in the two largest cities—Addis Ababa and Asmara.

Leaving education aside for the moment in order to consider it with other aspects of governmental activity, the next largest group is manufacturing, with almost 28,000 employees. Because of the strategic role of manufacturing in the modernization of the economy, it warrants closer inspection. Table 10 provides the relevant data for the last four years. We find first, as expected, an overwhelming concentration in the manufacture of soft goods—particularly textiles and foods—with only very small numbers employed in the output of other goods. Manufacturing has been growing at the approximate rate of 15 percent per annum. It should be noted that manufacturing, as here used, relates to firms with 5 or more employees.

TABLE 10

Manufacturing Employment by Sector

	1961–62	*1962–63*	*1963–64*	*1964–65* [a]
Total	*27,600*	*31,500*	*36,800*	*44,780*
Food	10,200	11,070	12,555	14,500
Beverages	1,350	1,565	2,580	2,800
Tobacco	450	460	445	450
Textiles	10,100	12,175	13,800	16,000
Leather and shoes	960	1,000	1,200	1,800
Wood industries	1,450	1,540	1,720	1,760
Nonmetal building material	1,290	1,280	1,290	2,760
Printing	400	550	800	1,000
Chemical	—	250	570	1,330
Steel, metal, and electrical	—	180	240	580
Other	1,400	1,430	1,600	1,800

Source: Planning Board Data
[a] Preliminary estimate.

Trade is an equally large segment, accounting for over 28,000 employees. The only other significant group outside of government is transportation, with 18,000 employees. Since trade is composed primarily of very small units which have little capacity for diversification and growth, the only significant modern sectors of the economy so far reviewed are construction, manufacturing, and transportation, which in the base year, 1962, accounted in total for about 110,000 or roughly one-quarter of the nonagricultural employment.

To this must now be added the substantial governmental sector with its large number of teachers, sizable number of administrators, and smaller number of health workers, comprising in total about 75,000 employees. The teachers and the health workers and at least some of the administrators belong to the cutting edge of the modern sector. But no matter how the data are stretched, we see that in the base year that the dynamic modern sector did not have in excess of 200,000 out of a total labor force of about 7 million, or roughly 3 percent.

Another way of assessing the relative strength of the modern sector is to estimate the several modern industries' contribution to Gross Domestic Product. The data for 1963 reveal the following shares:

	Percent
Manufacturing	2.5
Construction	1.9
Transportation	4.7
Education	1.0
Medical and health services	.8

As one would expect, the contribution of the modern sector in terms of output is considerably greater than in terms of employment, but the simple fact remains that in 1963 it accounted for only 11 percent of Gross Domestic Output.

This background helps to provide a base for estimating what lies ahead. As noted above, manufacturing has been growing at approximately 15 percent per annum. This is a rate considerably below that estimated in the 1962 plan. On the assumption that it continues to grow at this rate, it will account for 100,000 employees in the early 1970s

(1972–73). At that point, although its proportion of the labor force will have tripled—from .5 percent today to 1.5 percent, it will still be very low.

Using a longer perspective and a wider focus, it is likely that by the end of the century three-quarters of Ethiopia's labor force will still be in agriculture. And the more dynamic sector of industry, building and nonagricultural laborers, which today accounts for over 6 percent of the total labor force, will have risen, after a third of a century, to only 10 percent.

What would this order of growth imply for trained manpower? It would lead to an increase of professional, technical, and clerical workers from the very low .7 percent today to over 2 percent; and a corresponding rise in sales and commercial workers from 2.3 percent today to approximately double—4.6 percent at the end of the century. Since the total labor force would have expanded considerably, roughly from 7 million to between 15 and 17 million, these potential percentage increases imply a substantially enlarged absolute demand for trained manpower. But the increases from one year to the next will not be very large.

Before leaving these highly speculative projections we must note that they are postulated on a rate of growth of 5 percent per annum in GNP, which is of the order of 40 percent greater than recent experience; and they further postulate an annual rate of population growth of not more than 2 to 2½ percent. If either, or both, of these assumptions is found to be too optimistic, the transformation of the economy will proceed more slowly than here stipulated and the demand for trained manpower will be even more modest.

The implications for trained manpower of the potential growth of the manufacturing sector are suggested by the rough calculation that of every 100 new jobs, not more than 5 will result from a demand for administrative personnel including those with clerical skills. That means that if manufacturing should reach 100,000 by the early 1970s, there will be an annual demand for white-collar personnel of around 400 per annum. A considerable proportion of the latter represent positions that can be filled by high-school graduates or those who hold a two-year college diploma.

We have been dealing with those sectors of the economy that conventionally fall within the orbit of the "private sector," that is, where individual entrepreneurs play the critical part in deciding whether and how much to invest. We do not overlook the fact that in developing countries, such as Ethiopia, the government, directly or indirectly, tends to play an important role in the stimulation of the private sector through such diverse activities as providing a portion of the capital, guaranteeing against potential losses, absorbing the operating deficit for a number of years, or through other financial and nonfinancial assistance. It is very difficult in countries that are at the beginning of a modernization effort for private individuals to start without substantial assists from government, and it is one of the characteristics of advanced technological countries such as the United States, West Germany, and Japan that governments continue to play a prominent part in the stimulation of economic growth. But the order of dependence on government is much greater among those which are just beginning to industrialize.

Another word about the private sector in Ethiopia. It is important to recognize that with a small domestic market, with no clear comparative advantages, with high costs of transportation and power, with a scarcity of competent labor, the prospects for profitable investment in Ethiopia are restricted and are likely to increase only slowly as particular areas of specialization develop and as the costs of production are reduced. These cautionary notes about the barriers to the rapid expansion of the private sector are introduced to emphasize the fact that this sector offers little likelihood of any substantial or sustained demand for trained manpower in the years immediately ahead. Although this rather unfavorable conjecture of the future could be upset by discoveries of valuable resources within the country or by a radical change in the demand in international markets for products that Ethiopia could supply, neither eventuality appears imminent.

Against this assumption of a relatively slow growth in the private sector, attention must now be focused on the critically important governmental and quasi-governmental sectors. To begin with, it is important to note that government is by far the most important employer in the country; the military and police account for approximately 50,000 employees, and general administration, education, health, and other services have another 70,000. To this large number must be added the employees who work for such governmental corporations as electric power, telecommunications, highways, railroads, and airlines. There is no ignoring the basic fact that government dominates the nonagricultural sector of the economy. This domination has been, and will continue to be, crucial for understanding the demand for trained manpower.

For instance, a reference was made earlier to the estimate that not less than 95 percent of all those who have acquired a baccalaureate degree either in Ethiopia or abroad, a number estimated in excess of 1,500, work for government or for public institutions. Even if this proportion declines somewhat in the future—and such a decline is likely to be very modest in light of the anticipated slow growth of the private sector—the future demand for trained manpower, surely at the baccalaureate level and above, will be overwhelmingly determined by the intentions and capability of government.

What light can be shed on the nature of the demand of government for college graduates during the past several years and what lessons can be derived from current developments? It should be noted that government has been able and willing to absorb all college graduates at a stipulated minimum entrance salary of E$450 per month. Overwhelmingly, these graduates have been placed in technical and administrative positions in various ministries in Addis Ababa. The ministries of Education, Public Health, Finance, Community Development, and Agriculture have absorbed a high proportion of the total available supply.

Recently, because of growing budgetary stringency, tensions between the older, more highly placed non-college bureaucrats and the newcomers, and the lack of directly usable skills among many of the latter, the government has begun to be more selective. It still has unmet demands for many types of professional, scientific, and technical personnel—engineers, accountants, veterinarians, and other specialists. But it may be reaching a saturation point—if it has not already passed it—in its capacity to absorb usefully additional college graduates who do not have any type of specialized training.

The fact that most graduates are reluctant to accept a position outside of Addis Ababa and the fact that the government has had only limited success in overcoming their resistance will also affect its ability to continue to absorb ever larger numbers of new graduates. If more graduates were willing to accept positions in the provinces, the outlook would be more propitious for their continued absorption.

If the government proceeds with its plans to initiate a

widespread decentralization by placing responsibility for education, public health, road building, and community development at district level, and if it should start in fifty or so districts, there will clearly be a substantial demand created for trained personnel in addition to those who will be reassigned from national to district payrolls. But it would be very difficult to implement this radical program of decentralization, on so broad a scale, at one time, without prior experimentation and training. The government may therefore decide to move more slowly than its planning now contemplates.

Too much weight should not be given to the matter of the cost to government of hiring professional and trained personnel. The basic determinants lie elsewhere. With governmental expenditures currently at a level of E$456 million the cost per annum of hiring 250 graduates comes to less than $1.5 million or about three-tenths of 1 percent. On that basis, even a government in straitened circumstances could continue to absorb modest graduating classes for a long time to come. But there are additional dimensions, several of which have been suggested in passing, such as the desire of all graduates to remain in the capital, the incompatibility between many of the graduates and their less educated superiors, and the absence of a directly usable skill among many of the graduates.

Is there any point for the government to continue to offer employment to all graduates in light of these circumstances? Apparently the issue is slowly being faced, for there is scattered evidence that some graduates searched in vain for six months before they were able to find a berth. And some informed persons both in and out of the government are convinced that these signs of a more selective attitude on the part of government are harbingers of a trend. Current newspaper advertisements shed an oblique light on the situation: the government in announcing certain vacancies stipulates that either a high-school graduate with several years experience or a recent college graduate can apply. These may be straws in the wind but they are worth noting.

Although the absorptive capacity of government for college graduates with special skills may be relatively and even absolutely reduced in the years ahead, over the next five to ten years the outlook for college graduates in the liberal arts and sciences is not necessarily bleak—if they are willing to teach. We noted in the last chapter the substantial pressures that will be exerted on the educational system to expand, particularly at junior and senior high-school level. Attention was also called to the small number of Ethiopian college graduates in the school system—a mere ten or so. There is every reason therefore to postulate a large and continuing demand by the educational system for college graduates. The only question is whether, even in the face of declining opportunities for them in other branches of government, they will be willing to enter upon teaching careers. That is a matter to which we will direct our attention later.

We might also ask whether, in addition to education, there are not a great many important areas vital to the advance of the country in which there is currently a gross insufficiency of trained manpower—consequently a large and continuing demand. Take, for instance, health. Malaria takes an appalling toll; in the epidemic of the late 1950s at least 3 million were stricken and some experts estimate that over 13,000 died. Nevertheless, although the number of specialists and technicians is steadily being expanded, it is still far short of what is required to eradicate this debilitating scourge which, one expert has recently estimated, reduces the effective labor power of the country by about 25 percent. Present plans hope to bring this costly disease under control by the 1980s. There are a great many other diseases that also take very heavy tolls: intestinal diseases, trachoma, venereal diseases, tuberculosis, and nutritional diseases are but a few on a long list that result in excessive mortality and morbidity and a general lowering of physical and mental well-being.

What is available by way of health manpower to cope with these inhibiters of economic growth and human well-being? Table 11 sets out the total number of trained health and medical personnel in Ethiopia, exclusive of Eritrea.

A few observations will point up the unbelievably low ratios of trained medical manpower to population. In the nation as a whole (including Eritrea) there are 324 physicians, or 1 per 69,000 persons. Even this presents a more favorable picture than is actually the case. A high proportion of all physicians are in Addis Ababa, and all of the 29 licensed Ethiopian physicians are there. As far as the countryside is concerned, the ratio of physicians to population is about 1 to 200,000 and the entire group is composed of foreigners. The university, despite considerable uneasiness, recently established a medical school which has a current registration of 19. In addition there are 269 Ethiopians studying abroad in some one of the medical sciences. A minority are studying to become physicians, but it is unknown how many will return home upon the completion of their studies or when this will be. Under the best of circumstances no large increase in the number of Ethiopian physicians can be anticipated in the next five years or so.

The nursing situation parallels that of physicians. Here too, the national ratio of nurses to population is exceed-

TABLE 11

Health Personnel of Ethiopia, 1965 [a]

	Total	Employed by Ministry of Public Health	Employed Elsewhere
Physicians	319	149	170
Veterinarians	4	1	3
Entomologists	6	3	3
Sanitary engineers	8	4	4
Pharmacists	32	7	25
Asst. pharmacists	70	27	43
Radiologist engineers	1	1	—
X-ray technicians	49	33	16
Health officers	99	96	3
Community nurses	115	115	—
Sanitarians	95	94	1
Nurses	447	208	239
Midwives	62	34	28
Lab. technologists	20	16	4
Lab. technicians	90	70	20
Asst. lab. technicians	63	47	16
Dressers	2,170	1,381	789
Physiotherapists	8	5	3

[a] Excludes Eritrea.

ingly low, 1 to 52,000. Here, too, there is very heavy concentration in Addis Ababa. Here, too, the prospective outlook is bleak. Ethiopia is unlikely to graduate more than a total of 50 nurses annually over the next few years from its four civilian schools. There is, however, an important difference between the training of physicians and nurses. The major limitation on the expansion of doctors is qualified candidates. In the case of nurses this is not a problem: there were about 600 applicants for seventy places. But nursing schools, operated primarily by voluntary groups with little or no governmental assistance and support and with acute shortages of faculty, are in no position to expand rapidly.

The backbone of the Ethiopian medical service is the dresser—a man with as little as an eighth-grade education who has had one or two years of on-the-job training. With about 2,500 qualified dressers in the country, the resulting ratio is 1 to 9,000 persons. But again the distribution problem must be taken into account. Most of the dresser schools, operated more by voluntary groups than by government, are located in the southern and western regions. Dressers tend to work in the areas where they have been trained. Plans are now being made to establish schools in Harar and Gojjan provinces which do not have schools. The present annual level of output is about 240 graduates of the elementary course and another 110 who complete the advanced course.

The Public Health College of the university at Gondar, which began operations in the early 1950s, has produced a modest number of health officers, community nurses, and sanitarians. Today there is approximately 1 of each of these specialists for every 160,000 population!

Given these terribly small rates, we must ask what are the blocks in the way of an accelerated expansion of the supply to meet more effectively the needs of the Ethiopian population for health and medical services? Several clues have already been offered. It was suggested that the eradication of malaria will involve very substantial expenditures for many years. The government has estimated its capabilities for this program at around $3 million per year. The supply of potential candidates for medical school is very thin and in any case it takes time to bring a new medical school into full operation. The system of nursing instruction rests on a weak foundation. It lies substantially within the private domain, and the responsible groups are hard pressed to find the resources to expand.

But over and beyond these explanations there are two forces whose influence may be said to be determining. The Ethiopian people have a great need for a great many services, medical and other. But unless the consumer can find the money to transform his need into effective demand; or unless the government will step in and pay the costs of rendering the service, the public's demand will remain dormant. And, as suggested earlier, there are limits to the sums that the government can make available even for worthwhile services.

In addition, many Ethiopians do not eat enough, and what they do eat is not a balanced diet. Severe shortages of water and, equally important, lack of knowledge leading to misuse of the water that is available for drinking and washing often result in infection. In the face of these two major barriers to better health, it does not follow that a rapid increase in medical manpower, per se, would be the quickest or the best way to lower mortality and morbidity. Trained manpower is very short—but so are other basics such as money, food, water, and knowledge.

The same type of analysis can be followed through with respect to the nation's basic industry—agriculture—to show the need for much larger numbers of trained personnel to help raise the quality and quantity of farm output.

The two principal sources of trained agricultural manpower within Ethiopia have been the graduates of the Agricultural Vocational High School at Jimma (there is a second small school at Ambo) and the graduates of Alemaya, which now serves as the Agricultural Faculty of the university. Since approximately one-third of the more than 400 graudates of Jimma are currently students at the university and others have gone on to study and graduate from Alemaya, it is difficult to obtain a net count of those currently employed. An estimate of 400 high-school and college trained specialists in agriculture is reasonable. With 6 million persons engaged in agriculture, this provides a ratio of 1 specialist per 15,000, but this is a maximum ratio since about 200 are still in the educational pipeline. It should be noted that there are plans to convert Jimma into a junior college.

Once again, we can be quick to say that Ethiopia farmers, coffee producers, and cattle raisers could profit from much more technical assistance than this small group of technical advisers has been able to provide. But the matter is not so simple and the transformation of the latent into effective demand for additional technical assistance requires a host of adjustments. To mention only a few: in the absence of better seeds, more fertilizer, additional markets, the farmer can make little use of better information. The critical question is whether, given the small number of secondary roads, a substantial number of farmers could be effectively reached—even if many more specialists were available. Next, some of the potentially most fertile lands can be opened up for settlement only after malaria has been brought under control. And many other gains in agricultural output are closely connected with land reform and a basic reconstruction of traditional attitudes of behavior with respect to the ownership of cattle. Finally, the simple matter of budgeting support for a vastly increased agricultural extension service is also a problem of moment. The country surely can usefully absorb many more trained agricultural specialists. But the preconditions for their effective utilization will require both time and resources.

The question may properly be raised whether the preceding discussion on the structure of demand has not stopped far short of illuminating the specific types of trained manpower that an expanding Ethiopian economy and society will require. The answer is that great restraint was exercised in translating general assumptions about economic development into specific manpower dimensions. A review of earlier efforts of the Planning Board and by Professor Arnold Zach of the Haile Selassie I University indicated the great difficulties of such specifications. For instance, for the five-year period (1962–67) the Planning Board postulated a demand for over 1,800 professionals, 460 of whom were to be employed in manufacturing. Specifically it calculated a requirement for just under 300 engineers in manufacturing, of whom 120 were to be chemical engineers. As far as we were able to ascertain, instead of a requirement for 300 engineers, manufacturing has absorbed but a handful; and there has been no active requirement for chemical engineers! To take one more illustration: the plan saw a requirement for 470 economists, with 140 in manufacturing. The university output has averaged about 20 economists during the past three years. Clearly there is a wide gap between calculations or requirements and the numbers who become available or are in fact hired.

Professor Zach compared the 1964 employment of professionals and administrators with estimated requirements and availabilities for 1972. His table includes thirty-two categories. He calculated that in 1964 there were roughly 3,000 professionals and 2,000 administrators and that Ethiopians accounted for roughly half of the former and 85 percent of the latter. His requirements for 1972 are for over 8,000 professionals and 3,000 administrators. Aside from the inherent limitations of calculating requirements from employers' estimates of their future hiring intentions, these estimates cannot be related to anything that we know about the potential supply. Hence they must be viewed with great caution.

If detailed specifications about future requirements for trained manpower cannot be derived from economic planning data, what general conclusions can be drawn from this review of the structure of demand? A few points stand out. First, it is highly unlikely that the private sector, which has hired very few college graduates in the past, is likely to present an important demand for such personnel in the near future. We do not see the private sector growing, except at a very modest rate.

Second, the government, including quasi-government corporations, is likely to be in the future, as it has in the past, the principal employer of professional manpower. But here a shift is probably already under way which may be accentuated in the years to come. The government appears to have more and more need for particular types of technically trained persons—from engineers to physicians and less interest in employing college graduates with a liberal arts background for general administration. However, it has and will continue to have a large requirement for high-school teachers.

Government revenues have tended to increase since 1960–61 at the rate of 16 percent per annum compounded. Expenditures have kept pace. If the figures are corrected for the incorporation of Eritrea, the rate is reduced by 1 percent. These estimates include both extraordinary revenues and expenditures for the reason that we noted earlier that there is a commingling of both types of revenues and expenditures.

The financial position of the Ethiopian government in the years immediately ahead may take a turn for the better or conceivably even for the worse. But if, as is more likely, its expenditures continue to increase at a rate similar to that of the recent past, we can anticipate a steady but not spectacular increase in the demand for trained manpower. The specific nature of that demand will depend largely on shifts within the government budget. We will consider in a later chapter the outlook for expansion in education, particularly secondary education, which represents the potentially largest segment of the future demand for trained manpower.

We have seen that Ethiopia is at an early stage of development. The question arises, therefore, to what extent the major points that have emerged from this analysis of demand has relevance and pertinency for other developing nations, particularly those which are further advanced?

Development theory, like other theories, undergoes shifts and changes. Currently, agriculture, which was long neglected, has come to the fore. And well it might, since a nonindustrialized country cannot develop unless it improves its agricultural output. Otherwise there may not be enough food, and surely not enough surplus, to support development efforts in the modern sector.

But most developing nations cannot encourage even a part of their slowly growing supply of trained people to go into agricultural work. City-born and city-bred university graduates surely do not want to live in the provinces, and if a country boy has succeeded in escaping from the farm and has acquired a higher degree, he does not want to return to the backward countryside. Although the planners now realize the importance of high priority for agricultural reforms, it is another matter for government to encourage or direct the recently trained agronomist, teacher, veterinarian, or health official to take up residence in the countryside.

An important consequence of this difficulty of distributing the new supplies of trained manpower throughout the country rather than permitting it to concentrate in the principal cities is the relative speed with which the modern-sector demand for skills can be satisfied. Before long college and university graduates may find it difficult to obtain preferred jobs. In developing nations, government initially is the principal employer of trained manpower, but it soon reaches a point where, because of budgetary stringency, it can no longer add substantial numbers to the payroll.

Development economists used to believe that forcing the pace of industrialization would create a substantially enlarged demand for trained manpower, but they now realize that the expansion of output is likely to be very much more rapid than the expansion of employment in manufacturing and other modern sectors. As the modern sector expands, the demand for trained manpower will expand. But if three-quarters or more of the total labor force is initially anchored in agriculture, a great many years must pass before any large scale shift will occur in the occupational structure in favor of the modern sector.

Recently planners have calculated the "demand" for skills under varying assumptions of growth. Almost without exception, these forecasts have pointed to the absorptive capacity of the economy for a large number of trained persons with a wide range of skills. However, these calculations have not allowed for the failure of the development plan itself, for major shifts in the structure of the plan, for the brake that a slow growth of government income will put on the effective demand for skill, for the substitutability that exists between different types of manpower, and for the other factors that may undermine the assumptions or the conclusions derived from the extrapolation of particular trends. Manpower forecasting must be handled with great discretion in advanced economies; in developing nations it can be highly misleading. The effectiveness of manpower forecasting depends on the competence of the analysts to foretell the shape of things to come. Not many analysts have this competence.

✦ 6 ✦

Utilization

IN MANPOWER analysis, when studying the relations of supply to demand, we must introduce considerations of utilization. The adequacy of the present or prospective supply to meet the demand depends in considerable measure on the effectiveness with which people with varying orders of skill are utilized. But we must not establish as criteria levels of utilization which are not in harmony with those that have previously prevailed in the society or that we might reasonably anticipate in the future. If they are to be useful, considerations of utilization must be based on reality. And then they can add an important dimension to our understanding and can point directions toward constructive solutions.

Among the key parameters that are likely to determine utilization patterns are the policies and practices of large employers of trained manpower; wage structures and career opportunities that influence the allocation of manpower; relationships between particular groups such as between nationals and foreigners; institutional arrangements such as compulsory service, bonding, and subsidies that pull or hold people in one place rather than another;

and other mechanisms that affect the hiring, assignment, training, promotion, and discharge policies of employers in the private and public sectors of the economy.

One of the outstanding characteristics of the Ethiopian scene and one that has the most pronounced effect on the development and utilization of its trained manpower is the relatively high salary paid to the person who has acquired a college degree: a man with a baccalaureate degree is entitled to a starting wage of E$450 per month; one with a master's degree, E$550; and one with a doctorate receives E$750.

Since a student who finishes twelve years of school is likely to receive about E$200—and sometimes even less—as a starting wage, it is clear that the completion of the additional four years of college (now five years because of Ethiopian University Service) yields a very high differential return. And since college students are completely subsidized by government, the only cost to them of their remaining in school is the earnings they have foregone. Moreover, since employers are not eager or able to absorb large numbers of high-school graduates without specialized competence, the foregone earnings of the college group must be set at a low figure.

Let us compare the annual salary of a man newly graduated from the university with the earnings of a skilled factory employee. The factory worker may earn E$1,000 annually; the recent college graduate received five and a half times as much. What is the relative productivity of the two and is this connected with the substantial wage differential? Such a direct comparison is practically impossible, but perhaps we can shed some oblique light on it. Since the overwhelming majority of college graduates are employed by government, let us attempt to determine how well are they utilized.

We have noted that most of the senior officials in positions of authority are likely to have had less formal education than the recently hired college graduate and that this fact alone often creates tensions between the two. Superiors frequently do not know how to make good use of the young men assigned to them. Moreover, they are frequently unable or unwilling to provide them with the orientation and in-service training which a newcomer must have if he is to do his job. And if a man gets into the habit of not working, or not working to capacity, he may soon be unable to work well.

Additional difficulties within the governmental structure militate against effective utilization of the recent college graduate. The department may be short of funds and therefore unable to launch or carry through programs to which the better trained younger people could make a distinct contribution. Because of the delicate political balances that must be maintained at and close to the top, many senior officials understandably are loath to delegate any responsibility to the younger members of their staff, especially is they do not have reliable supervisors. Since power is tightly held by the minister and a few associates, many young people are left for long periods of time with no specific assignments, or with assignments which have little significance and less urgency.

To complicate matters still further, the determination of all young college graduates to find a berth in Addis Ababa greatly reduces the possibility of their receiving assignments in which they could make good use of their skills.

Another characteristic of the governmental structure is that it has been found necessary to shift senior staffs frequently among the different ministries—that is, ministers come and go, and vice-ministers likewise are moved around. While such movement is in the nature of all organizations, and particularly new or rapidly expanding organizations, the fact remains that instability at the top carries a price throughout the organization. It makes it difficult for those in the middle of the hierarchy to know how to conduct themselves. They are likely to be preoccupied with their relations to their superiors. This leaves them with less time to guide and direct those who report to them.

These strictures do not imply that all young graduates languish upon entering government service, but there are substantial and not easily negotiable barriers that prevent many young people from performing with their true effectiveness. If, however, they come to the government with some technical education—in engineering, economics, or health—it is more likely that they will be slotted into positions where they will be afforded an opportunity to make use of what they have learned and, equally important, be in a position to add to what they have learned.

One more characteristic of the civil service structure warrants attention. Despite the relatively frequent changes at the top, current policies look with disfavor on mobility at the bottom. Once a man has accepted a position in a ministry, he is not free to leave either because he is dissatisfied or because he has located a better opening. He can leave only with the express consent of his supervisor. And since many officials are unsure of their positions and believe that turnover in their staff may be interpreted as a failure on their part, they are frequently reluctant to grant this permission. Knowing this, the young man often does not even seek it. While excessive mobility can be a drawback, the present situation seems unequivocally to be characterized by too little mobility to assure effective utilization.

What about the absorption and utilization of trained manpower in the quasi-governmental organizations and in the nonprofit and private sectors of the economy? First, note should be taken of several circumstances that differentiate these organizations from conventional government agencies. The former tend to have somewhat more flexibility with respect to hiring standards and wage structures. They tend to be much more responsive to the market. Next, they rely to a much greater degree on foreigners to provide leadership and direction. In many instances, foreigners hold down all of the strategic positions in the organization. Since their goal is to provide goods and services, these organizations are more directly concerned with in-service training and other approaches that can contribute to the more effective utilization of their trained and trainable manpower. Moreover, several of these organizations are sufficiently large and diversified that they are able to develop a career system, including the rotation of men from less to more desirable locations. Since this is known, they encounter less difficulty in assigning new members of their organizations to locations where they may not want to live but where they will have a better opportunity to make a contribution through using their skills and potentials.

Some of these organizations, such as the Ethiopian Airlines and the Highway Authority, recognizing that they could not possibly meet their responsibilities without heavy reliance on foreign skills and know-how, have developed short-term and long-term contractual arrangements with foreign companies to help them meet their high priority programs.

Some indication of the scale and significance of on-the-job training programs is reflected in the following selected data. Ethiopian Airlines currently has a training staff of 16 instructors with an approved program aimed at doubling the staff. Currently, the technical trainers are about equally divided between Ethiopians and Americans, and as the staff expands and Americans are added, there will be provision made for Ethiopian counterparts. Last year, 1,800 men received technical training, an increase of 15 percent over the preceding year. Fifty Ethiopian technicians hold 80 internationally recognized licenses, and the present expanded training program aims at the early phasing out of TWA.

During the last nine years the Highway Authority has run 36 different programs covering all phases of its work, varying in length from two weeks to nine months and involving about 3,000 employees.

The Ethiopian Electric Light and Power Authority has also sponsored a series of in-service training programs since 1960–61, for the most part directed at selected employees with ninth-to-twelfth–grade education. While the numbers trained have been relatively small, totaling between 30 and 50 per year, the programs have been of relatively long duration, most of them between one and two years long.

Since liberation, Ethiopia has had a much more friendly stance toward the use of foreign specialists than many other developing nations. Since the country had never been under colonial rule, it apparently suffers fewer complexes. It is probably correct to say that most of the professional, managerial, technical, and skilled manpower on which the modern sector depends has until very recently been provided almost exclusively by foreigners.

An estimate made by the Minister of Interior in 1962–63 and brought up to date by using special census data for the twenty-three principal cities indicates that the number of foreigners currently in Ethiopia approximates 50,000. About half are Europeans and half of the Europeans are Italians. The Middle East accounts for slightly more than a third, all but a few stemming from Yemen. Thus, about 2 out of every 3 foreigners in Ethiopia are from either Italy or Yemen. The Americas, primarily North America, account for 5 percent, and approximately the same percentage is accounted for by Asians from other countries than those in the Middle East. There are a thousand or so individuals from other parts of Africa.

Many Yemenites live in small towns and villages while other foreigners are concentrated to a marked degree in Addis Ababa and Asmara. These two cities are the residence of half of the foreign population in the country. About 20 percent of all foreigners are in smaller cities, primarily those with a population of over 20,000.

In recent years, the Ethiopian government has required resident foreigners to have work permits. Since the law was promulgated, slightly over 5,000 permits have been issued. As one might expect, men received 90 percent of the permits, women 10 percent.

Except for the Yemenites, the foreigners are a well-educated group. Of those with work permits, 25 percent are college graduates, and an additional 50 percent have graduated from high school. Because upper-class Ethiopians have long avoided commerce, it is not surprising to find that almost one-third of all foreigners are in commerce, followed by slightly more than one-quarter in manufacturing. Services, construction, and transport together account for about another third. Agriculture (mostly plantation farming) and utilities together account for the remaining 10 percent.

Further evidence of the strategic role that foreigners are playing in the modern sector of the Ethiopian economy is in the salaries and wages which they earn. The median wage of registered foreigners is E$650 per month, considerably above what most Ethiopian college graduates earn. Even more striking is the fact that fully a quarter of all registered foreigners earn over E$1,000 monthly and a small minority—5 percent—over E$2,000!

Two broad conclusions can be drawn from the above: the majority of college-trained men in Ethiopia are foreigners; and foreigners, college-trained and other, play key roles in commerce, manufacturing, construction, and in most professional and technical services.

We have already considered selected wage and salary data, but we will now review such information as is available to illuminate the development and utilization of the nation's human resources.

Table 12 sets out the range of salaries and wages that are currently paid in various sectors of the economy. A first inspection reveals that most wage rates are exceedingly modest in consonance with the low level of per capita income and the early stage of the nation's industrial development. Agricultural workers receive E$10 a month; custodial workers, E$30; production workers in manufacturing receive E$40; and most of the working population falls within those groups.

But in the modern sector, there is a different level of salaries. A diversified group of clerical, skilled, and semiprofessional workers receive E$200 to E$250 monthly. And there we find that master electricians, mechanics, and plumbers can earn up to E$1,000 monthly—the salary of a minister! A skilled stenographer can command E$700 and, if bilingual, even more.

Restricted as the modern sector is, these figures indicate that there is a market for skill in Ethiopia and that employers and the public are willing to pay well for competence. The wide spread between the wages received by skilled workers and those earned by master craftsmen,

TABLE 12
Wages and Salaries by Skill Level, 1965

	Monthly Rate	Daily Rate
Professional and executive		
Ministers	E$ 1,000+	
Those with doctorates	750+	
Director-Generals	700+	
Those with Master's degrees	500– 550+	
Those with Bachelor's degrees	450+	
Provincial governors	150+	
Civil Service		
Administrators	450–1,000	
Subprofessionals	75– 525	
Clerical and fiscal help	40– 375	
Trades and craftsmen	40– 375	
Custodial and menial workers	30– 125	
Semi-Professional and technical		
Master mechanics	400–1,000	
Master electricians	400–1,000	
Master plumbers	400–1,000	
Commercial school graduates	300– 700	
Nurses (diploma)	250– 375	
Skilled carpenters, masons	200– 250	10–12
High-School graduates (diploma)	200	
Advanced dressers	120– 220	
Hotel workers (higher level)	100– 200	
Elementary dressers	90– 150	
Skilled and semi-skilled		
Skilled workers, factory	50– 80	2–3
Production workers, industry	40	
Peripheral dressers	30– 60	
Mechanics, electricians, plumbers (starting)	25– 30	1
Laborers, building trades workers		1
Unskilled		
Wonji Sugar Estates workers		1.00–1.10
Indo-Ethiopian Textiles workers (Addis Ababa)		.90–1.00
Factory workers		.80–1.50
Bahar Dar Textile workers		.65– .80
Agriculture laborers		.30– .70

which is also evident in the difference between bottom and top wages in the clerical field, emphasizes once again that it is a high order of competence that is in scarce supply. Apparently there are many who can do certain aspects of a job, but only a few can do them all.

There are several important implications for manpower policy that flow from these data. While an increase in the supply of skilled and partially skilled persons is certainly called for and will yield a net increment to the economy above the cost of training, the real challenge is to train more people to a high level of competence. This is not easy, especially in light of the limited number of potential trainers, but special attention should be focused on this important objective.

We do not want to leave this table without calling specific attention to the low salaries for provincial governors. Although the data are not shown, there are other key positions in government where the starting salary—or even the maximum salary—is strikingly low. Since certain officials are unable to discharge their functions effectively unless they live at a certain level—and since men of talent will not be drawn into certain lines of work unless they see a prospect of supporting their families at a reasonable standard of living—a governmental wage scale that is grossly out of line in some fields may either discourage good men from entering or staying in certain lines of work, or perpetuate unfortunate practices whereby they can augment their salaries. This is not a sound foundation for a modern state and a progressive economy. Although the government will not find it easy to allocate additional revenues to the end of correcting gross salary anomalies, it should make every effort to do so. In any case, it would be better to have a few officials with ability and integrity than a large number of mediocre ones who cannot support themselves on their salaries.

We have noted that the majority of secondary school teachers in Ethiopia are foreigners, and that members of the U.S. Peace Corps and contract teachers from India account for the predominant number. But relevant to the present discussion of utilization are the difficulties inherent in this system, in which many poorly educated Ethiopian principals are in leadership positions with respect to two or more streams of faculty personnel which in turn have more points of difference than of similarity with regard to their preparation, approach, and techniques. In a great many instances, although fortunately there are exceptions, the contribution of these foreign teachers is much below what it might be were there more rapport with the leadership and among themselves. But one of the heavy costs that Ethiopia must pay is that it must tolerate so much slippage among these scarce manpower resources.

This situation is not limited to secondary schools. At the primary level also there is considerable tension between teachers and the administration. The conflict is not solely one of nationality and culture but also of age and outlook. The younger, more modern, and better trained teachers, for the most part graduates of the teacher training institutes, are frequently in conflict with their principals who tend to be conservative and reluctant to approve or even tolerate innovations. Many young teachers, instead of receiving the guidance, help, and support from their supervisors which they desire and need to become more experienced pedagogues, are forced to shift for themselves and at times are prevented from doing a good job.

While there are a great many disadvantages to teaching as a career, this source of difficulty ranks high in Ethiopia and goes far to account for the substantial turnover that is found among teachers. To make matters worse, the turnover tends to be heavily concentrated among the younger, abler teachers who refuse to become ground down by the system. While the Ministry of Education is seeking to upgrade the existing administrative corps and to refine its selection and promotion procedures for administrators, it is seriously restricted in what it can do by shortages of competent personnel, limited resources for training and upgrading, and by the imperatives of the situation which force it to make use of most of those who today hold supervisory posts.

A recent survey revealed the following list of reasons that teachers decide to withdraw from the profession and seek alternative employment: administrative inefficiency, including delays in receiving salaries; unprofessional working conditions; lack of opportunity for self-improvement; geographic isolation; low prestige of teachers; adverse living conditions; and low salaries.

Clearly, there are a great many factors that have an adverse effect on teachers as they see the circumstances of their work. The above listing also implies that no one nostrum is likely to solve the problem of widespread dissatisfaction which leads to a high rate of turnover.

At the university level, a related set of problems can be identified. At both the administration and faculty levels there are Ethiopians, Europeans, Americans, and Asians, each with differing philosophies of education. The determination to expand the university rapidly necessitated such a potpourri, but there is no escape from paying a price in lowered effectiveness. During the last fifteen years of its existence, Alemaya has had about 250 graduates, all but a few of whom are Ethiopians. In recent years, an effort has been made to accelerate the Ethiopianization of the teaching staff and lately the administration.

We undertook a special survey of the 224 Ethiopian graduates of Alemaya in February, 1966, and obtained information about all but one. Our object was to test the validity of oft-heard criticism that many of these graduates were not in agriculture and, particularly, were not working in the provinces. The 224 total was reduced to 220 through death or emigration, and further reduced to 177 by virtue of the fact that 43 were currently studying abroad.

The occupational ties of the 177 disclosed that about 60 percent were directly connected with agriculture, 25 percent indirectly; and the remainder had shifted to another field of work where, however, many were utilizing at least some of the knowledge and skills that they had acquired at Alemaya, such as statistics, chemistry, or economics. If we subtract the 20 who were teaching at Alemaya, the remainder were roughly divided between those working in Addis Ababa and those in the provinces.

There is no simple way of determining—surely not from these data alone—whether, and to what extent, the Alemaya effort can be adjudged a success. Since there are 6 million farmers in the country, it would be easy to say that after fifteen years to have only 75 graduates working in the countryside is too few, too slowly. But it is difficult to see how the stream could have been very much larger considering the objective which was to establish a strong agricultural college. The open issues with respect to Alemaya relate to the objectives, training, implementation, and the speed with which Ethiopianization has been pursued. Also relevant to all discussions of utilization are the relations between the faculty and the Ministry of Agriculture, which recently took over from Alemaya responsibility for the extension service.

The finding that 43 Alemaya graduates are currently studying abroad leads into another aspect of utilization. This relates to the question of who goes abroad for study,

what they study, and what happens to them on their return. As might have been anticipated, information about
those going abroad is considerably better than about the
returnees.

The first point is that approximately 1 out of every 3
Ethiopian college graduates was educated abroad. There is
a widespread impression among informed persons that
those returning from overseas and seeking government
employment in recent years have been at a disadvantage.
They apparently face difficulties in readjusting to Ethiopia
and in reknitting their ties; and in turn those in authority
appear to be wary about young people who have been long
exposed to foreign ways of thought and action. This is
flagged as an issue on which further study might prove revealing and rewarding.

The most recent data—1965–66—reveal a total of 1,557
students residing abroad. The following summarizes their
distribution by major field of study:

Social Sciences	330
Medical Services	269
Engineering	255
Education	173
Agriculture	164
Humanities	113
Fine Arts	53
Natural Sciences	38
Military	19
Unclassified	137

The United States, in which 305 students are studying,
leads the list, followed by Italy with 174 and Germany
with 138. The following countries each have a hundred or
so students: Lebanon, United Arab Republic, USSR,
France, and the United Kingdom. The remainder are scattered widely through other Eastern European, Asian, and

African countries with small numbers in the Western Hemisphere outside of the United States.

Unfortunately, the data do not reveal the proportion of students who are pursuing diploma-level work (junior college) , baccalaureate, or post-graduate training. Since in recent years the Ethiopian government has sought to establish strict controls over the outflow of students, it is a fair inference that a high proportion of the total group, especially those who have left recently, are persons who have already acquired their baccalaureate degrees or are studying in a field in which the university does not offer a program.

Once again, there can be no doubt that Ethiopia has benefited from the opportunity of so many of its young people to study abroad, especially in former years when the university was just getting organized. But the availability of a large number of scholarships for foreign study is not an unequivocal benefit. We must remember in this connection that government salaries are geared closely to the employee's level of formal education. That means that many individuals find it to their interest to obtain a foreign scholarship or fellowship. In addition, those who have already been overseas as well as those who have only heard about the outside world through their friends are often strongly drawn to spending time abroad.

There is considerable evidence to suggest that many young people make their career plans around the possibility of foreign study. They may take a job in a ministry which has relatively little need for their training because they believe that their chance of getting abroad is better. And others prolong their stay abroad for reasons more connected with their personal aggrandizement than with their possible contribution to the economy and society at home.

It can be argued that a substantial reduction in the outflow of personnel for foreign study might result in a considerably higher utilization of the nation's trained manpower. This proposition may hold up even if full allowance is made for the long-run contribution of an individual who has acquired advanced training. Competition among East, West, and the neutral countries to entice ever larger numbers for study is not necessarily of advantage to Ethiopia. If this competition among sponsoring countries continues, the Ethiopian government should act to tighten controls over those who go overseas, for how long they go, and for what types of study. In reaching decisions about these matters, the government will want to assess carefully the potential long-run gains from additional study for trainees against the short-run losses incident to their disappearance from important agencies and assignments.

Increasing the supply and deepening the qualifications of educated and trained manpower is a major axis for improving the quality of the nation's manpower resources. But the burden of this chapter has been to highlight some of the important factors governing the utilization of such manpower which has the capacity to stretch the supply or to waste it.

Actions leading to the more effective utilization of scarce manpower resources can prove as profitable and sometimes more so than those directed to increasing the supply. A 10 percent improvement in the utilization of a supply of 1,000 educated and trained persons is likely to be the equivalent of an entire year's addition to the supply.

In developed as in developing economies, utilization is the most neglected facet of manpower. When politicians or scholars perceive a present or potential gap between demand and supply of trained personnel, their response is in terms of expanding the supply. They tend to ignore or discount the possibility of improvements in utilization.

Now there is some justification for underestimating the potentiality for altering patterns of utilization, since these patterns frequently are deeply ingrained and do not readily yield to efforts at reform. For example, it is quite difficult in advanced societies to bring about significant changes in the utilization patterns of physicians, teachers, or other groups of professional personnel.

Tradition is one barrier; the self interests of various groups is another. But there is more to the story. The salary and wage structures that prevail in the different markets for manpower, public and private, as well as current recruitment, assignment, promotion, and separation policies exercise a powerful influence on the ways in which manpower resources are distributed and utilized. Frequently the interplay between these market and institutional forces and the utilization of manpower is not understood.

Several distortions of the appropriate wage-productivity relations are characteristic of many developing countries. In the first instance, teachers and first- and second-level administrators are frequently paid much more than they could demand in open bidding. They benefit from a lag in the wage mechanism which does not yet reflect the much larger numbers who have recently been trained. The result is that those who already have jobs are overpaid, while many equally or more competent do not have jobs or must accept jobs at markedly lower wages.

Another distortion is the result of the relatively large numbers of people who have acquired some order of skill but who cannot carry a job through from the beginning. There are very few individuals in the public or the private economy who can cope with the many complex facets of a complete assignment. In the private sector, the truly competent people are likely, sooner or later, to command a wage or salary commensurate with their productivity. But in the public sector such expertise will be harder to demonstrate; and it will seldom command appropriate rewards.

Underlying these difficulties is the tendency of most developing countries to assess the worth of a man not by what he can do but by the education and training which he has undertaken and the degrees which he has acquired. Without sound systems of performance evaluation, this is an understandable substitute and one which, incidentally, is used in many developed countries as well. Increasingly, professional salaries in the public sector—in teaching, social work, science—are geared to the education that a man has acquired.

This overemphasis on formal education as the hallmark of competence carries with it a neglect or downgrading of the importance of learning on the job and even from more formally structured efforts. We know what many developing nations are short of competent supervisors. But from the viewpoint of manpower development and utilization, it would be preferable to meet this deficiency head-on rather than to go around it.

No matter how well young people are educated and trained, if they are not effectively supervised much of their skill and potential is likely to run to waste. The classroom can only help prepare a man for work. Much of what he needs to know he must learn on the job—and he can do this only if he works for somebody who can help him grow.

Among the costly errors that many developing nations have made is their failure to establish a sound policy for the replacement of foreigners, many of whom have the skills and competence necessary to be effective supervisors. Some countries have not put a training demand on these foreigners; others have acted precipitously in removing them and putting the local population "in its place." The first error results in a waste of training capacity; the second is an invitation to institutionalizing incompetence. Both carry a high cost.

But even when the developing nations perceive the importance of using foreigners to help them build up the competence of their own people, the leadership must do more if the training is not to run to waste. The Civil Service must see that men are placed and kept in positions for which they have been trained. Some able men will have to be assigned and reassigned to positions of greater importance and responsibility, but the personnel system must be sensitive and attuned to the challenge of effective utilization. If politics and nepotism determine assignments and reassignments, manpower wastes can reach appalling heights.

✦ 7 ✦

Education and Manpower

THE LAST decade has witnessed a burgeoning of world-wide interests in the relations between education and manpower. In technologically advanced economies this has taken the form of ascribing to education the substantial margin of gains in output that cannot be explained by inputs of labor and capital. The "residual" gain has increasingly been interpreted as reflecting improvements in the quality of the labor force, which in turn have been ascribed largely to improvements in education. In their less sophisticated contentions, protagonists of education's contribution to rapid economic growth have simply resorted to correlational analysis: they have presented data to show that increased expenditures for education have been accompanied by substantial economic growth, and that countries experiencing the fastest rates of growth are usually those which have devoted the largest absolute and relative shares of their governmental budgets and total national income to education. They find that countries which have been falling behind in the economic race are for the most part those which are underspending on education.

Most students who are concerned with the problems of development in the less industrialized countries are similarly enthusiastic about the contribution of education to economic development. They sometimes emphasize literacy; sometimes "high-level manpower," a concept which includes professionals and administrators together with those with intermediate-level skills. This approach stipulates that accelerating economic development depends on enlarging the nation's supply of educated and trained manpower, which in turn depends on broadening and deepening the educational system.

It is not necessary to quarrel with this formulation to make the simple but important point that the analysis is too general to be of much help to policy-makers. Sir Arthur Lewis, among others, has sought to add sophistication to the discussion by introducing such variables as the absorptive capacity of developing societies for different types of educated persons as well as the relations between their wage and salary levels and their economic productivity.

This chapter will raise to visibility a range of considerations affecting the relations between education and manpower, some of which have already been touched upon. Unless the underlying complexities of the relationship are made clear, there is the danger that one of two oversimplified approaches will be accepted as doctrine. On the one hand, the protagonists of more education of all kinds without consideration for the absorptive capacity of the economy and the society might carry too much weight. Or else, those who contend that estimates of present and future manpower requirements alone should determine the size and contours of the educational system might determine policy. It will be the thrust of the following analysis that both positions are untenable and that the criteria to be employed must be more sophisticated if major errors in policy are to be avoided and valuable resources saved.

We will begin with some general observations about the role of education in the general development of Ethiopia and follow them with a more focused discussion of problems affecting elementary and secondary schooling; then we will consider some special problems of higher education. If the analysis appears to be some distance afield, it will be eventually tied back to manpower.

One of the principal instruments for welding Ethiopia into a more unified whole is through the diffusion of public education with its stress on the use of Amharic as the basic language of instruction. Since this effort should also contribute to the broadening of the market and the quickening of the economic pulse, those who advocate that education at the primary level should be expanded only slowly, if at all, will have to prove their contention. The cautionary group points out that wastage is high because many pupils drop out before reaching a minimum level of literacy, that lack of qualified teachers is a severe bottleneck, and that the government's financial position cannot stand the strain.

Arguments in favor of expanding elementary education are strong even beyond that which assumes expansion to be essential to nation-building. We know that in the foreseeable future many children will not reach the fourth grade and only a small proportion of those who do will ever reach the seventh or the ninth grades. But the size of the pool available for junior and senior high school is closely related to the expansion of the elementary school. Only if the first grades are enlarged, will the numbers of qualified entrants to junior and senior high school be increased. And certainly the development of Ethiopia requires larger numbers of junior and senior high-school students than are presently or prospectively in the pipe line.

As to the teacher shortage, a serious problem exists but it may not be insoluble. No nation in the throes of a rapid educational expansion will ever have the number of qualified teachers it needs or desires. The only way for an expansion program to succeed is through expedient compromises. We have noted that Ethiopia succeeded in raising significantly the quality of its teaching personnel over the past decade. While currently many teachers do not have the desired education and skill, only a doctrinaire argument would state that it would have been preferable to gear the expansion of the system to the availability of fully qualified teachers. A more reasonable approach would be to recognize the problem of teacher supply as a major challenge and to seek ways of increasing the supply as expeditiously as possible.

Now to the question of costs. One of the most interesting recent developments has been the willingness of many rural communities to take the initiative and build a school in the hope and expectation that the government will provide a teacher. If economic development requires the transformation of unemployed and underemployed rural labor, here is evidence of such a transformation. It should be encouraged so that eventually rural labor can add a wide variety of infrastructure—roads, sanitation, silos, as well as education.

Of course the erection of a school building, frequently with materials furnished in part by government, does not relieve the pressure for operating budget once classes begin. But if rural people want a school it may be possible for them over time to help carry at least part of the costs. While the rural population is generally very poor, not every region is equally poor. Moreover one reason for widespread poverty is the lack of hope of rural people which acts as a brake on the fuller deployment of its efforts and energies. Fiscal caution is a desirable stance but it should not be turned into dogma.

There is a further reason to favor the expansion of basic schooling at a faster rate. The major keys to development lie in altering the conditions of rural life. If agriculture is to be improved, if debilitating diseases are to be brought under at least partial control, if isolated villages are to be linked with small towns, if people are to learn about personal hygiene and sanitation—in short if they are slowly to develop a new stance toward themselves, their children, and the future—they must have an opportunity to learn. There can be no significant gains in agricultural productivity, in health and sanitation, in roads, and in the expansion of the money economy without a simultaneous educational revolution which will provide the foundation and support for these and other changes. The broadening of basic education in the countryside is a *sine qua non* for economic development.

Because of the difficulties of expanding education in the rural areas as rapidly as would be desirable, no resource, actual or potential, should be neglected. In this connection we call attention to the fact that in 1964–65 about 22,000 pupils in church schools were following approved government curricula. The Ethiopian Church Office reports that at present there are 1,557 local church schools with 1,684 teachers and 53,902 pupils, primarily in Shoa, Arussi, and Hanar provinces. These data indicate that most church schools are one-teacher institutions. Moreover, only half of the pupils entering church schools with government-approved curricula enter the second grade and less than a quarter survive to the fourth grade. Clearly, the productivity of the system is limited.

But there is another dimension. The priests' schools are attended by many children in their fifth year. Almost half of the boys and a quarter of the girls in Addis Ababa between the ages of 5 and 9 have attended these schools where they learn to read and recite the traditional prayers in Gez. There may be more potentiality in church and priests' schools than has yet been explored. One approach might be to attempt to up-grade the teaching staffs of the church establishment.

The implicit argument in the foregoing discussion has been that instruction in reading, writing, and calculation —together with a modest introduction to history, geography, and the world of nature—would help introduce subjects into the traditional culture which would have a dynamic effect on the thought-ways and behavior patterns of the rural population.

Ethiopia should seek to profit from the errors committed by other developing nations which did not consider the curriculum in relation to the occupational aspirations of their growing student body. Most students considered school as the avenue of escape from the rural areas, as a road to white-collar positions in government. But no government with a rapidly expanding school system has been able to absorb the large numbers of partially educated who have fled from the countryside. If Ethiopia is to avoid the frustrations which result from the unrealizable occupational aspirations of the oncoming generations, it must seek to relate junior and senior high-school curricula more directly to the needs of agriculture and the activities closely related to agriculture.

Junior high schools will provide terminal education for a high proportion of the expanding student body. Hence the question of how the subjects in which they provide instruction can be significantly related to the way of life of those who will remain on the farm or in small communities closely linked with the agricultural hinterland must be considered. While each student should acquire the foundations for further learning—primarily competence in reading and calculation—whenever possible the curriculum should be infused with illustrations and applications to local agriculture and the environment of rural life. The school can and should make a significant contribution to raising the levels of health and sanitation as well as agricultural productivity. It can go a step further and seek to prepare selected students to assume beginning positions in health or agricultural extension work by the end of their ninth year.

The same general principles should be followed with respect to senior high schools. Here, too, planning should aim at providing terminal education for a high proportion of the expanded flow after teaching them the basic tools for further learning. As noted earlier the Ministry of Education should early seek to introduce a second type of certificate which would attest to the fact that a student has satisfactorily completed high school without regard to his suitability for college.

For both those who leave school at the end of high school and those who pursue further education, mastery of English is essential. There will be little opportunity for young people to advance in the modern sector of the economy unless they have access to the knowledge of the West, which in Ethiopia means knowledge of English, sufficient knowledge to read speedily and comprehend.

In this context English represents the core of significant vocational preparation. Conventionally "vocational" relates to the manual and mechanical arts and skills. Current planning contemplates the staffing and operating of a large number of comprehensive high schools in which students will be able to pursue different curricula but where many will select training in such fields as carpentry, plumbing, electricity, motor mechanics—skills that are in very short supply at the present time. Planning also contemplates the training of instructors for these fields in recognition of the fact that very few are currently available. Finally, planning recognizes that the capital and operating costs for such curricula are quite high and special commitments have been obtained from the United States to assist in carrying the extra financial burden involved.

This brings us to the university. It is a primary responsibility of a university, especially a national university which stands at the apex of the educational system, to safeguard the cultural heritage of a nation. Further, it must keep itself open to all branches of knowledge and research out of which the future will be fashioned. To respond too narrowly to the pulls of the moment, to be overly responsive to current and prospective manpower needs as defined by various interest groups, would be a betrayal of its trust. A university that does not adopt and maintain the long view will not long remain a university.

But these imperatives are not enough. There are important considerations involved in the more effective use of costly academic resources—facilities, faculty, student time —that must be reviewed so that sound policies can be defined.

Our earlier analysis points in the following directions. The university should exercise great caution in expanding its enrollments because the high attrition rate indicates the desirability of first improving the quality of the student body. Moreover the limited nature of the potential pool underscores the desirability that the university refrain from establishing any new schools or major departments in the near future. If particular specialists are in short supply, such as veterinarians, it would be preferable to have students trained abroad.

The earlier discussion of Alemaya suggested that the number of graduates for the fifteen-year period was very modest. Considering the expensive nature of the facilities at Alemaya, its large faculty, and the absorptive capacity of the nation for more agricultural and related specialists, we recommend that a two-year diploma course for agricultural technicians be developed at Alemaya. We further recommend that consideration be given to establishing a closer relation between Alemaya and the Teacher Training Institute at Dira Dawa with an aim of expanding the institute or developing a junior college, or both. The substantial educational plant at Alemaya must be reorganized so that it can make a larger contribution to the output of trained manpower, particularly in light of the teacher shortages.

An inspection of the university catalogue reveals a proliferation of courses. This is confirmed by a study of enrollment data by course. But proliferation is costly, not only in terms of faculty utilization but because it contributes to imbalance in learning. A college should provide an opportunity to obtain instruction in fundamentals and in the more important advanced branches of knowledge. Narrow specialized offerings have little or no place in a college curriculum. Early efforts at consolidation of the curriculum should yield significant gains both in the utilization of faculty time and in student performance.

The university has had to piece out its faculty from among representatives of a great many different academic traditions. The effective coordination of diverse strains is always difficult. While there is no possibility that the university will be able to escape from heavy reliance on foreign staff in the foreseeable future, it may make significant gains if it can attract and hold for somewhat longer periods of time men of recognized academic competence. A smaller staff of able people who serve for longer periods is definitely to be preferred to a larger, more heterogeneous group with short periods of service.

One of the most interesting and constructive developments of the young university has been the establishment and expansion of its Extension Division. This division operates at three main levels: it provides degree work in arts and business, various diploma and certificate programs, and a correspondence course in secondary education. Table 13 shows the distribution by locality of the 1,640 extension students. The predominance of Addis Ababa in the total complex stands out. In the past decade, exclusive of law students, 62 extension students earned their baccalaureates, 115 secured certificates, and 6 earned diplomas. In the law program, 48 are enrolled in the second year of the diploma course; 25 in the second year of the degree course; and 17 will soon earn their degrees, making a total of 90.

The armed services and the police as well as other government departments and agencies have furnished a considerable proportion of the extension student body. Many of these agencies as well as certain private organizations pay the fees for their employees who enroll.

In a country where the opportunities to complete secondary school and gain admission to the university have been exceedingly limited, especially for young people from outlying areas, the availability of another route into higher education is very important. If much valuable talent is not to be lost, many need a second chance. Although communication difficulties place severe limitations on the speed with which extension can expand and although there are other limitations related to staffing and administration,

every reasonable effort should be made to broaden the
scope of the programs by offering extension courses in the
major centers in the country and by adding to the courses
as conditions permit.

TABLE 13

Enrollment in Extension Programs, 1965

	Number of Students
Total	*1,640*
Addis Ababa, Arts	1,120
Addis Ababa, Engineering	112
Addis Ababa and Asmara, Law	190
Asmara	109
Debre Zeit	54
Dire Dawa	40
Harar	15

We must now consider the central issue: What are the
implications for educational planning that can be extracted
from the present and prospective manpower situation?
Let us first recall the major caveat with which this section
was introduced—that the building of an academic curriculum at university level must not be determined solely in
terms of manpower criteria. We will then revise our question: What if anything can manpower criteria contribute
to university planning?

A cautious first response is that if there is a danger of
flooding the country with college graduates for whom
there would be no suitable employment, as in fact has occurred in a great many Asian and Latin American countries, action should be taken in time to slow the inflow and
encourage those who are admitted to reconsider their fields
of concentration. But there does not seem to be serious
danger of a substantial excess of college graduates in Ethi-

opia in the near future if the recommendation advanced
earlier of expanding enrollments modestly is followed.

This leads to the more difficult problem of the distribution of students among faculties and departments. There
are two contrasting ways of approaching this problem. One
is to contend that manpower planning should determine
the numbers to be trained in each field; the other holds to
a laissez-faire concept in which students are free to make
their own choice—at least as far as existing capacity permits
—and to rely on feedback information from the market to
correct gross errors.

We hold no brief for the former but neither do we
believe in a completely laissez-faire approach. The key factor is this: young people differ in interests and capacity;
they cannot be treated as homogeneous units.

Next, college should stress both general and specialized
aspects of education. It is hoped that the engineering student will learn something more than engineering, and that
the arts student will probe one or another field in depth.
Another important consideration is that a great many positions in the public and the private economy require men
of competence but not necessarily men with a specific type
of training. To illustrate: it is often a matter of indiffer-
ence to a business organization whether a young man has
concentrated on statistics, economics, or accounting as his
field of specialization. The employer may not even care
whether the applicant had selected chemistry or marketing
as his major field. What he really wants to know, if he is
doing a good screening job, is whether the young man has
learned his subject well, has demonstrated analytical
strengths, and has a flair for problem solving. For such a
young man will have the flexibility to meet any reasonable
assignment. He has learned how to work and has demonstrated an ability to do so.

Therefore the question of how students should be distributed can be answered by saying that as long as each department provides a curriculum which is analytically oriented and where the students must demonstrate that they can think and solve problems, the distribution of students is unimportant. Students are not irrational. They are not likely to study fine arts if they look forward to working in a bank, nor will they concentrate on French language and literature if they hope to work for the Ministry of Community Development.

What problems remain? If year after year the market is searching for additional engineers—and if the university has the capacity to increase its enrollments without undue strain—it would be desirable to encourage, through counseling and other devices, a larger inflow into engineering. But analysis would have to show a continuing need. Moreover, the need might be for electrical or mechanical engineers. There might be no current or prospective demand for chemical engineers. One thing is clear. The responsible university officials must keep a close and continuing contact with the principal employers.

To consider the obverse, there might be relatively little demand for graduates in science. But even if there were little likelihood of any change in the near future, the university would not close down the major science departments. However, counselors could explore with the interested student body whether and under what conditions they would be willing to enter secondary teaching, where they are sorely needed, or what applied skills they might add to their science major which would heighten their employability in other sectors. For instance, a science major with a strong minor in statistics might be easy to place.

There is no need to expand these examples. The rele-

vant points stand out clearly. Effective university planning
should aim to allow maximum freedom of choice to the
student. Next, strong guidance and counseling services
should be available. The responsible department representatives must devote time and energy to keeping abreast
of the changing structure of demand for their graduates
and must institute a follow-up system so that they have
some hard facts to go by. The most important challenge
that the university faces is to establish and maintain standards which will insure that all of its students demonstrate
the ability to deal analytically with problems in their
chosen field.

If an effective feedback system is established between the
market and the university—and it is difficult to foresee any
barriers that would prevent it—the distribution of students
should be determined by the students themselves. Many
are not sophisticated when they enter the university, but
by their junior year they should be able to make responsible choices, especially if the university fulfills its obliga-
tions with respect to information gathering and the provision of guidance services. Many students may make mistakes, but the point to emphasize is that any alternative
system will also permit mistakes. And the probability of
errors would be greater under an approach grounded in
such an illusive concept as national requirements for specific skills.

The burden of this analysis has been that while there are
significant connections between education and manpower,
the connections are never simple and direct. There are
fundamental values associated with decisions about the
scale and scope of the educational system that transcend
narrow considerations of manpower and even broad considerations of economic development. Education has a
capacity to alter the terms of life even if it raises per capita
income only slightly. Education has an instrumental value,

but its basic worth is its contribution to enlarging the horizons of the individual and the nation in addition to its specific contributions to increasing the nation's output of goods and services. The basic issues of education cannot be solved in manpower terms although the manpower dimension has a role to play.

If national manpower considerations should not determine the shape of the educational system, personnel and money will largely determine the scale and scope of the educational system. To these we now turn. To deal with the money first. In the decade between 1957–58 and 1966–67, total governmental expenditures for education increased from a level of about E$17 million annually to about E$64 million, or an increase of just under fourfold. During this same period, government's total expenditures increased from about E$175 million to E$530 million, or roughly threefold. The current budget provides that education receive about 14 percent of the total—up from less than 10 percent a decade earlier.

Table 14 presents the details of the education budgets for 1965–66 and 1966–67. The very large increase of 24 percent must be read in light of an interim adjustment upward of about E$5 million in the 1965–66 budget which makes a net increase for 1966–67 over 1965–66 of about 14 percent. The most striking fact about this table is the very substantial increase over the twelve months budgeted for primary schools.

If government expenditures continue to increase until the end of the decade at the same rate as they have in the past, and if the current proportion of 14 percent continues to be allocated to education, what level of funds will be available in 1968–69 for education? The approximate figure is E$93 million, or just under E$30 million more than in the current budget for 1966–67. Depending on actual government revenues and the proportion that education will receive, the actual figure may be somewhat higher or lower. But we believe that this is a reasonable estimate if past trends continue.

TABLE 14

Education Budget, 1965–66, and Proposed Education Budget, 1966–67

	1965–66	*1966–67*
Total, All Education	E$51,865,806	E$63,882,386
Total Government Expense	35,266,714	43,551,430
Ministry and Overhead	1,779,853	1,828,753
School administration	1,654,718	1,672,718
Primary schools	6,208,592	11,266,368
Secondary schools	5,423,183	6,612,473
Technical and vocational schools	1,692,758	2,131,634
Teacher training institutes	1,071,004	1,385,648
Adult education	722,666	750,242
Foreign scholarship grants	1,256,000	1,000,000
Grants to pupils, local schools	842,870	—
University scholarships	100,000	50,000
Payments to Peace Corps and EUS	718,000	1,327,524
Grants-In-Aid, autonomous institutions	250,000	279,000
Haile Selassie I University	8,547,070	10,247,070
Total, External Assistance	16,599,092	20,330,956
Peace Corps	7,500,000	9,000,000
Technical assistance	1,748,092	2,480,593
Secondary school teacher training	658,000	658,363
Vocational training	—	752,000
Haile Selassie I University	6,693,000	7,440,000

The E$63.8 million education budget for 1966–67 provides for expenditures for the following major categories:

Overhead and other	E$ 5,252,000
Primary schools	16,266,000
Secondary schools	4,628,000
University	17,737,000
	E$63,883,000

If these sums are divided by the number of students—
admittedly a very crude method—the annual cost per student is:

Primary schools	E$	45
Secondary schools		450
University		7,500

Thus, a university student costs the government per year
166 times as much as a student in a primary school and 16
times as much as one in secondary school.

Let us now calculate the probable costs of the proposed
increased enrollments which were reviewed in chapter 4.
It will be recalled that two sets of estimates were presented: those which we calculated on the basis of the historical trend and those in the IDA plan. We anticipated a
much slower growth in primary schools and a more rapid
growth in secondary schools than did IDA. Our dollar estimates for 1968–69 amounted to a requirement of E$21
million for primary school and E$41 million for secondary
schools; or a subtotal of E$62 million. The IDA figures
are, respectively, E$27 million for primary schools and
E$36 million for secondary schools, or a subtotal of E$63
million.

We calculated the university's budget on the basis of a
net increase in the freshman class of 150 a year, which appears to us to be a reasonable estimate of a compromise
among the pressures for admission; the nation's need for
more trained manpower, particularly high-school teachers;
and the urgent requirement that the university improve
the quality of its student body in order, among other ends,
to cut its high attrition rate. On the basis of an additional
intake of 150 per year, the university budget for 1968–69
will require just over E$22 million.

How does the estimated rise in total education costs

compare with the estimated rise in revenue? This is how
we see it:

E$ Million

Overhead	6	
Primary schools	24	(average between IDA and historical trend estimates)
Secondary schools	40	(historical trend estimate slightly reduced in light of IDA)
University	22	
	92	

If the anticipated revenues of E$93 million become
available for education, the increased enrollments stipulated above can be handled, that is, the money will be
there. One question remains: What about the teacher supply?

Once again, it may be helpful to begin with the current
supply and see it against the perspective of the recent past
before introducing calculations about the near future. In
forecasting data about teachers, we will have to specify the
level of teaching to which we refer. However, it should be
noted that frequent changes in the organization of the
school system, particularly between grades six and nine,
make it difficult to establish comparability over time.

During the last two years, there was a net addition to the
teacher supply of slightly less than 600 per annum, about
equally distributed between elementary and post-elementary teachers. For the analysis which follows, we distributed the available teacher supply for 1965–66 among the
following three levels of the school system:

Primary schools: Grades 1–6	8,090
Junior high schools: Grades 7–8	823
Secondary (including vocational) schools:	
Grades 9–12	1,274
	10,187

The determinants of future supply are the present supply, less attrition, plus additions from the teacher training institutes and the Education Faculty of the university, plus other sources, domestic and foreign. On the basis of past experience an attrition rate of 7.5 per annum appears reasonable. It should be observed, however, that the graduates from the teacher training institutes have an attrition rate of perhaps as high as 15 percent per annum.

In the following estimates we have used established teacher-pupil ratios, although we have allowed for changes over time. In addition, these data refer to the formal system as a whole and extend beyond government schools per se.

Once again, the different estimates of future student enrollment are crucial in our attempt to define the future of the educational system, this time with respect to the need for teachers. The IDA plan sees that the supply of primary school teachers must increase from 8,090 in 1965–66 to 12,934 in 1968–69, or by 4,844. Our historical trend data suggest a net additional requirement of 2,370. Since calculated attrition will roughly equal the net addition of teachers from the teacher training institutes, under the IDA estimate, about 1,600 additional teachers will have to be obtained from other sources for each of the next three years; with our more modest estimates the requirement from other sources will be for slightly over 750 annually.

However not even half of this requirement—350 additional teachers—has been secured in any one year from "outside sources." To meet a 750 requirement will be a major challenge, and to reach a goal of 1,000 or more annually will be exceedingly difficult if standards are not to be completely sacrificed.

The situation with respect to junior high-school teachers, while on a much smaller scale, is equally stringent.

Here, an increase of about 400 to 500 on an 800 base will
be required. However, attrition will far exceed the net increment that will become available from the university
diploma recipients who in 1968–69 will still number
under 50. Therefore between 220 and 250 junior high-
school teachers will have to be secured from "other
sources." This is almost double the number that has as yet
been attracted in any one year.

The high-school situation calls for an increase of between 700 to 900 teachers by the end of the decade on a
base of less than 1,300. Even using a lower attrition rate, 5
percent, the losses from the supply of secondary school
teachers will exceed the degree graduates in education
from the university by a wide margin. Using the more conservative IDA enrollment expansion estimate, an annual
requirement of about 250 high-school teachers from other
sources is established, and using our estimates, the requirement will rise to about 375 new teachers annually. Once
again, there is no evidence that the government will be
able to meet a requirement of this magnitude without very
special efforts, if then. Although over 250 high-school
teachers were added in each of the two last years, the predominant group were members of the Peace Corps, and
the other large contingent were students on Ethiopian
University Service. There is little or no prospect of further
additions from the Peace Corps of this order of magnitude,
and the gain from the Ethiopian University Service was in
the nature of a one-time increment. Therefore, foreign recruiting remains the principal prospect for large additions
from outside sources.

The foregoing analysis indicates unequivocally that
even if governmental financing of education remains gen-
erous, it will be exceedingly difficult for the country to
meet its educational targets. Since the requirement for

teachers for primary schools is large, substantial short-run improvization will be easier in the face of budget leeway and the ever-larger numbers of better educated people in the country. If, as is likely, the government will compromise on standards, at least for the short run, a considerable expansion of elementary education can take place even in the face of a teacher shortage. It will be possible to attract at least partially trained persons into the classroom.

More difficult situations are found at the junior and senior high-school levels. Here the principal opportunity for increasing the teacher supply lies in attracting liberal arts graduates into teaching and seeking to entice many returnees from foreign study into the high-school system. Foreign recruiting offers the only other major potential source of teachers.

It should be noted that the "teacher crisis" may begin to ease at the beginning of the next decade when the number of graduates from the teacher training institutes will be considerably larger as will also be the number of diploma and degree candidates who complete their work in education at the university. But if Ethiopia is to press ahead on its educational front it must continue to do its utmost to expand the supply of teachers at all levels and, equally important, seek to retain a larger number in the profession.

Since the Western world has been arguing about the purposes of education ever since the subject was precipitated by the Greek philosophers, it is not surprising that there is no consensus among many countries in Asia and Africa about the goals of their educational systems and the articulation between that system and their efforts at industrialization and economic development.

In recent years there has been substantial agreement that the colleges and universities of these developing nations should not be pale imitations of London and Paris.

This much has become clear. But much else remains shadowy. Certainly the emphasis on quality—the hallmark of the university systems of Western Europe—has relevance for any educational system. One cannot blithely ignore it.

Similarly, it is not easy to jettison a British prototype and to replace it with that of an American land-grant institution. The established institutions are not likely to give way without a major struggle and most of the new countries cannot run a new parallel system.

But irrespective of the model, other basic problems remain and one is directly related to the analysis at hand. Should the educational system in these developing countries be responsive primarily to the emerging needs for trained manpower or should it develop and modify its plans with only incidental consideration given to present and prospective manpower requirements?

There is widespread evidence of the dangers inherent in a failure to align the educational system and the nation's economy. To train large numbers of liberal arts graduates and large numbers of lawyers for whom there are only a limited number of positions is a waste of resources from the viewpoint of the individual as well as the community —and can undermine whatever fragile political and social stability a nation may have established.

But if to ignore the question of how graduates are to be fitted into the economy is an error, the opposite approach —that of dovetailing the educational system closely to the economy—may be an equally great error. We have noted earlier the great difficulties, in fact, the impossibility, of forecasting manpower demands with any order of specificity. Therefore the economic and educational planners must not presume too much. But they should aim to assure that all who pass through the system, especially at the higher levels, will at least have the analytical and related tools that will facilitate their absorption into any one of many different sectors of the economy. Most important, their education should contribute to their willingness to go where their skills are needed.

A second area of recent intensive discussion has centered around the amount of resources that a developing country should devote to expanding its basic educational system. The initial position held that education was a good, and that any reasonable expenditures on broadening and deepening the educational system were justified. The more recent argument has been that limited resources can be wasted by expanding elementary education too rapidly. The effort can absorb a great amount of resources and the corresponding yield in the output of trained manpower may be quite small—among other reasons because of the substantial attrition along the way. This is the present-day sophisticated view: education at the lower levels should be expanded only gradually.

But the economic value of investments in education cannot be measured solely in terms of trained teachers and professionals. Most developing nations are tradition-bound agricultural societies. Unless the farm population alters its way of life, development will fail. Education is the one dynamic factor that holds some promise of changing the status quo. It cannot do the job alone, but without it little in the countryside is likely to change.

There is evidence in many developing countries that poor as the farm population is, it is usually able and willing to make substantial sacrifices to provide schooling for its children. This means that all of the costs of expanding education need not be a charge against the budget of the national government.

The question of expanding education is of course not simply a matter of money and buildings. Teachers are a critical resource, supplies and equipment another. But in the matter of teachers, as elsewhere, poor countries must seek to strike a balance between quantity and quality. It is well to remember that even in the most affluent countries in the world not all teachers meet prevailing standards. If the output of the educational system is being expanded relatively rapidly, it is likely that the quality of the teacher supply at the elementary level will inevitably rise.

One of the most difficult challenges that the planners face in developing countries is to obtain statistical control over the flow of students through the educational hierarchy so that they can learn where efforts at improved articulation are required. In some countries, the capacity of the colleges and universities is excessive relative to the number of qualified students who are admitted. In other areas, such as in South America, the situation is the reverse. The numbers admitted to the university are very much larger than can be effectively educated and trained. As a consequence, the attrition rate is appallingly high, with corresponding waste of economic resources and deep personal frustration.

If the burgeoning educational system and the expansion of the economy are to be kept in balance, special efforts must be made to learn about the employment and career prospects of the graduates in order better to structure and restructure the curriculum. This holds at every level of the educational system—from rural schools to the university pinnacle. The aim of education should be to broaden the realistic options of young people without raising their expectations beyond a reasonable point. Education should be a dynamic factor, but it should not create a class of marginal persons who can no longer fit into the environment into which they were born and brought up and who cannot make a place for themselves in the advanced sectors of the society.

✦ 8 ✦

Leverages

THE WAYS in which people prepare themselves for work and life, the education and training which they seek, the jobs and careers which they enter, the places to live—in short the whole range of decisions with respect to how to develop skills and use them—is heavily conditioned if not overwhelmingly determined by the structure of the society and economy in which they grow up. It is the opportunities they face—as well as the barriers they must surmount—that dictate the channels they follow as well as those they eschew. Finally, the rewards that attach to different types of work, both in terms of current wages and future prospects, have a strong influence on the decision-making process of most individuals.

If they have real alternatives, most men will pursue the kind of work for which the monetary and non-monetary rewards are greater. Therefore, in any broad consideration of manpower strategy, it becomes important to consider the ways in which the key determinants that influence the actions of individuals and groups with respect to the development and utilization of their skills tend to operate in order to evaluate whether changes in some of them might result in a higher level of utilization of the nation's human potential. It is important at the same time to determine whether certain changes might result in the more economical use of the nation's scarce resources which must be deployed in the development process.

There is no logical way to deal systematically with a host of distinct mechanisms which have a present or potential impact on manpower strategy. Here a simple bifurcation will be followed. We will first treat with those mechanisms that are related to education and training, and second with those that are more directly involved in wage structures and career systems. It matters little whether certain ones which overlap are treated under one or the other rubric, since it is the analysis, not the ordering, that is important.

To begin with education: On the assumption that it is desirable for the government to adopt a positive stance toward the continuing expansion of elementary education, we believe that the present modest efforts of the government in providing communities with building materials, if they assume the responsibility of erecting a school, should become firmly established as a policy as quickly as possible. In order that the budgeting requirements implicit in the more rapid expansion of basic schools should not outpace the government's ability to meet this added burden, it is recommended that priority be given to those communities willing to take on some proportion of the expenses involved in the operation of the new school. Depending on what happens with the current proposal to decentralize responsibility to the districts for education and certain other basic services, it may be possible to effect a change which over time will shift more of the burden for local school financing from the central government to the local taxpayer. Certainly the potentialities of such a shift should be carefully explored from two viewpoints: a higher order of local interest and involvement and a potentially greater yield in revenue.

Since the rate of school expansion depends greatly on increases in the teacher supply, we recommend that consideration be given to the early establishment of several additional teacher training institutions, especially in provinces which today lack such facilities. An effort should be made to have the Peace Corps contribute what more it can to the interim staffing of these new institutes.

Table 15 presents information about the staffs of the teacher training institutes and their level of educational preparation. Several points become clear: first, the important role that foreigners play in the staffing of these critically important institutions; next, the significant contribution of the Peace Corps volunteers; third, the fact that a majority of the Ethiopian staff do not have baccalaureate degrees; and fourth, the presumptive evidence that there is scope for enlarging the two smaller institutions, particularly since Harar has the reputation of a highly effective establishment.

Consideration might also be given to the potentialities of enlarging the other existing institutes. But accelerating the expansion of basic education does not depend solely on enlarging the output of teacher training institutes. The steady expansion in the numbers of the population who have completed high school or gone beyond, as well as those with between nine and twelve grades of schooling, means that the total available supply from which grade teachers can be obtained is substantially greater than is generally realized. Admittedly many of these prospective teachers will be less well trained than would be desirable. But there will be at least a partial compensation in that they may be hired at a somewhat lower wage than fully qualified teachers, which will help keep down the costs of

TABLE 15

Staff of Teacher Training Institutes by Level of Preparation

	Total	Addis Ababa	Debre Berhan	Harar	Asmara
Total	86	25	14	30	17
Ethiopians	34	10	9	8	7
Master's degree	3	3	—	—	—
Bachelor's degree	12	5	2	2	3
Less than Bachelor's degree	19	2	7	6	4
Peace Corps	27	4	3	16	4
Master's degree	10	2	—	6	2
Bachelor's degree	17	2	3	10	2
Less than Bachelor's degree	—	—	—	—	—
Other	25	11	2	6	6
Master's degree	13	5	1	3	4
Bachelor's degree	9	4	1	2	2
Less than Bachelor's degree	3	2	—	1	—

the expansion. To assure those who are distressed about relying on unqualified teachers, it might be added that more can be done to assist them through the preparation of better teaching aids and through various types of in-service training opportunities.

One area where the elementary school teacher needs a great deal of help relates to the more effective instruction in Amharic in those regions of the country where people speak another tongue. Improved efficiency in language instruction would yield a substantial increase in the productivity of the entire instructional effort. Another area where assistance is needed is the teaching of English, which involves all who teach in the junior and senior high-school system. Once again, gains on this front—particularly with

respect to effective teaching of reading comprehension—
could yield very large overall gains. Investment of talent
and money and an effort to secure foreign assistance in ac-
complishing these objectives should be accorded high priority.

Experts often think of education primarily or even
exclusively in terms of the development of literacy. While
intermediate and advanced education can be built only on
a foundation of literacy, it does not follow that the very
large numbers of nonliterate persons—in Ethiopia, the
overwhelming majority of the population is nonliterate—
can be ignored in educational programing. This would
surely assure a low rate of return on money invested in
educating the young. Educational reform in a traditional
society must bring about a change in the orientation of the
whole population towards its problems. And to accomplish
this, the nonliterate adults and the children who are being
turned into literate citizens must be brought forward together.

The most potent method available for the instruction of
the nonliterate is the radio. A single transistor can serve a
relatively large number of rural people. It can provide
them with a range of useful information about life in their
own community and how it might be improved, as well as
broaden their horizons about conditions in the larger
world outside. It can entertain as well as instruct. Much
more consideration should be given to the potentialities of
using radio as an instrument of adult instruction.

Currently young people are attracted to higher education and to specialized training through the pull of the following: free board and room, pocket money, free tuition,
and the prospect of a preferred position upon satisfactory
completion. There are, however, two negatives that go
along with these positive charges. College students must

devote a year to Ethiopian University Service, and those who enter the Laboratory School and the Education Faculty must give their bond that they will serve as teachers for two years for each year they received government support. Many of the specialized training schools also have bonding arrangements.

The first observation about this complex of incentives and commitments is the understandable need of government and quasi-government organizations to secure some direct return from their outlay of sizable sums in educating and training young people. The more specialized the training, the greater the potential loss, unless a man eventually uses his skill on behalf of those who underwrote his training. The telecommunications agency could not plan and program its work unless it could look forward to employing, at least for a period of years, those whom it has laboriously trained to varying orders of efficiency. This obtains in varying degrees for other public bodies with specialized missions both in the military and civilian sectors.

Since the period of instruction in the specialized training schools is usually considerably shorter than a full university program, since the bonding arrangements are often one year for each year of subsidy, and, most importantly, since the wages that a trained man is able to earn approximate even if they do not equal the market rate, the bonding arrangement is more formal than oppressive.

But the matter is quite different when it comes to prospective teachers. First, of all university graduates, only teachers are bonded. University students must devote one year to Ethiopian University Service, which adds to the length of their preparation. Perhaps most important is the dissatisfaction that so many prospective and actual teachers develop when they compare the wages and working conditions in their field with those in other fields. A high

proportion feel that they have made the wrong choice.
Faculty members of Haile Selassie I University report that
it is not uncommon for education students to plead for a
failing grade since that is one way they can escape.

Aside from questions of legality, equity would determine that it is difficult to justify holding an education student for eight years or longer, while no other students are
subject to bonding. Another objection to bonding is that
teaching, like other professional careers, requires a degree
of interest and commitment on the part of the individual.
How much are children likely to learn from a man who is
disgruntled with his work and is seeking the first opportunity to escape?

In addition, while harassed government officials who
face acute manpower shortages may believe that relief lies
along this line of capturing and holding people, in point
of fact such a procedure is likely to deflect attention from
the most serious needs, namely, to establish a meaningful
career system which will be sufficiently attractive so that
most qualified teachers will want to remain within the
field of their choice.

Now there are several serious shortcomings to teaching
as a profession as it is currently organized in Ethiopia. We
noted earlier that many teachers complained about the
weakness of many administrators who fail to provide educational leadership and who frequently prevent their putting forth their best efforts. In addition, low salaries, delays
in the payment of salaries, reinforced by the low status of
the teacher in many communities, are further drawbacks.
Finally, we must call attention to the fear of many teachers
that if they are once assigned to the provinces, and especially if they land in a very small community, they are
likely to be forgotten. In a country such as Ethiopia, where
conditions of life in smaller communities are very much

less attractive than in the larger centers, this fear is a real one. It also explains why, in one way or another, a considerable number of teachers have in the past escaped from the profession upon graduation without ever setting foot in the classroom.

While remedies are not easy to develop, nor will they be inexpensive, the directions where remedial action should be sought are reasonably clear. The government should back off from the discriminatory bonding of students of education just as quickly and as completely as possible. Its ability to do this will be enhanced if it introduces the changes outlined below concerning stipends and related matters. Next, it must expeditiously develop a career system, together with firm commitments to put it into effect. Young teachers must know that if they are assigned to a small village for an initial period of two to three years, they will, upon evidence of good performance, be reassigned at the end of that time to a more desirable location. Consideration should be given to the use of monetary incentives to compensate for hardship posts and to build other incentives into the system.

A true career system must also provide the opportunity for a few to qualify for various types of advanced programs which in turn are the gateway to better positions. Moreover, a higher degree of objective assessment must be introduced into the selection of individuals for administrative positions. It would also be helpful to introduce, as soon as the manpower resources permit, a small number of technical and professional consultants whose principal duties would be to visit provincial schools and to give support and assistance to the young teachers who are isolated.

We recognize that all of these recommendations require additional money and trained manpower, both of which are scarce. But the net additional investment may be much

less than the gross. Currently the government is operating
a teacher-training–assignment system with a great many
holes. It is forcing more in but the net annual addition to
the supply is quite modest. For instance, last year when 650
qualified teachers were graduated, the supply showed a net
gain of only 150. During the year 500 experienced teachers
left the system.

It would appear, therefore, that if the current widespread dissatisfaction of members of the teaching profession and of those in the process of preparing for a teaching career is to be dissolved and replaced by a positive attitude, the government must move in the directions outlined above. Otherwise any prospect of sound and successful educational expansion will be jeopardized.

As we have stated, the elimination of bonding will be
easier if the present approach to student stipends is altered.
Currently, the university pays all costs, including living
costs, for every regular student admitted. There are several
objections to such a procedure. Some part of the student
body is surely able to pay part of their living costs, and a
minority can cover all the charges and meet their living
expenses. In a country where money is urgently needed to
meet a large number of high-priority objectives, to subsi-
dize people who do not require subsidy is a poor use of
public monies.

What about the much larger numbers of students who
have no family resources? Is it not logical to continue the
present system for these students? And if, as appears likely,
they are the majority, will the effort to make other changes
be worthwhile?

The answer is that on two grounds—economic and
psychological—major changes should be introduced. Young
people work hard to reach the university and to complete a
course of studies because they know that substantial ad-

vantages will accrue to them after graduation. Currently they are assured a minimum starting wage of E$450 per month. Therefore, a baccalaureate degree is a valuable asset which has considerable earning potential. Under the circumstances it seems reasonable to suggest that the young people who will benefit from attending the university should make some economic contribution toward the acquisition of this valuable asset.

The reasonable way to do so is to require that they obtain loans for some part of their collegiate expenses. Once they begin to earn a salary, the period of payback should be long enough so that it will not impoverish them when they are establishing themselves, but it should not be stretched out beyond a decade or so. Since most graduates will work for the government, it should prove to be a fairly simple matter to deduct the appropriate monthly amounts from their pay.

The establishment of a system of part scholarship and part loan as a method of payment for college would have additional advantages. The government might find it desirable to consider partial or total forgiveness of their debts if individuals are willing to enter certain fields of work or are willing to accept difficult assignments. For instance, special consideration might be offered those who are willing to teach for a stipulated number of years, particularly in outlying areas.

The approach has flexiblity. The subsidy component might be varied if it were found desirable to attract a limited number of additional young people into certain fields where the course of studies offers more than average hurdles, i.e., engineering, or where other resistances to entry must be broken down.

All of these advantages are more or less evident once they have been detailed. But there is an important psychological reason for moving in the direction of having the individual pay a part of his way. Too many students, once they have been admitted to the university, believe that this is all they have to do, that henceforth they will be rewarded for this simple fact of college entrance. They feel that they are entitled to a degree, to a good job, to the perquisites that go with good jobs. They stop working just when they should begin to work in earnest. But if they must bet on themselves, if they recognize that access to higher education is a privilege, if they acknowledge the necessity of self-discipline, their approach to their studies and their careers is likely to be much more serious and constructive. There is something inherently antagonistic between total economic dependency and intellectual independence. The two do not meld. A man who is paying his own way—at least in part—owns his own soul.

So much for education. Now a few words about training. No matter how much the educational system is expanded and improved, increases in skill and competence will in large measure depend on the effectiveness with which different types of training are carried out. The major difficulty that all developing nations face is the lack of an adequate group of competent trainers and training situations. In addition, in Ethiopia, many in the training stream lack the ability to read the training manuals, which are available only in foreign languages. These deficiencies loom particularly large in the training of noncommissioned officers in the army, but they have their counterpart in the modern civilian sector.

Every effort should be made to overcome the insufficiency of good trainers and training situations. This means that all contracts with foreigners authorizing them to undertake work on their own account or on the account of the government should include a commitment to undertake to train an optimal number of Ethiopians as part of their mission. Such a commitment will involve additional costs, but the government will not be able to duplicate as cheaply the opportunity to add to its supply of skilled manpower by making full use of competent foreigners who are working in the country.

Along these same lines the government should review critically the numbers and types of persons who are being sent abroad for training to discover whether it might not be practical, in a considerable number of cases, to reverse the procedure and bring one or more competent persons to Ethiopia for a sufficiently long period so that they could help to upgrade partially trained Ethiopians. On balance, it is usually better to train a man on his job than to transfer him to a totally different environment. When a man goes abroad, he must make two radical adjustments: to the new environment, and later, when he returns home, he must adapt what he has learned.

Ethiopia is less xenophobic than most developing nations because it was never a colonial possession. But there are signs of an increasing amount of restiveness on the part of various branches of government over the hegemony of foreigners over so many advanced sectors of the economy.

We do not recommend that the authorities discourage the entrance of additional competent foreigners or speed the exit of those who are in the country, but rather that they insist that those with skill and competence assume a continuing obligation to train Ethiopians. This training responsibilty should be placed on all foreigners who are in a position to discharge it irrespective of the needs of their own concerns. Further, this responsibility should be placed on the small but growing number of Ethiopian establishments who have a training capability. Before a decision is made as to how to implement this recommendation, it would be desirable for the Manpower Resources Division, considered in the tenth chapter, to undertake an inventory of existing industrial and related training potentialities.

Related to the foregoing is the question of whether the government should move to establish a formal system of certified apprenticeships. Once again some preliminary investigations would be in order to determine the feasibility of such a system at this time. The key consideration is whether a sufficient number of good training situations can be found and whether effective government-labor-employer cooperation could be elicited. This much, however, is known from our earlier analysis. The number of master craftsmen is very small, judging from the wages they are able to command. This suggests that more highly skilled and broadly competent craftsmen are needed and could be absorbed. The question is whether the capabilities to train them already exist. This should be the focal question for an inquiry.

This brings us to the third and last category of leverage points—those which relate to wages and the market. Attention was directed earlier to the fact that Ethiopia has followed the practice of gearing wages, especially for new appointees, to their level of education. In the absence of other readily available methods of wage determination, this is a reasonable approach. Therefore, we do not argue against continuing for the time being the current procedure which establishes—at least for the governmental sector—a fixed relationship between entrance wages and educational achievement. It will be necessary of course to test from time to time the validity of the scale against the nongovernmental sector of the economy and to make adjustments if necessary.

But a wage structure that is geared to educational accomplishment should not be extended throughout the entire range of jobs. We believe that early action should be taken to make automatic salary increases independent of the possession of higher degrees—the Master's or the doctorate, as is the current practice. A much preferred approach would be to develop a salary scale for positions requiring different levels of complexity and responsibility and to establish independently the qualification for such posts. It is the level of work that should determine the wage, not the level of a man's educational background. If this shift is made, it would have many benefits, including a restraining influence on the indiscriminate pursuit of additional education by members of the bureaucracy. Too many people today go overseas for study for no other reason than to assure themselves a higher salary when they return to Ethiopia.

Admittedly, a shift from tying wages to educational accomplishment opens the door to nepotism and other improper bases for selection and promotion. Great care will have to be exercised by the responsible government agencies to insure that selection and promotion are based on merit. This will require in each instance a careful appraisal of the applicant's prior performance and his potential to meet the demands of the new job. Objective measures of assessment will not be arrived at easily, and there will be errors in the procedure even if great care is exercised to avoid all sorts of improprieties. But a developing economy in which the governmental sector looms so large cannot afford to follow the present unsatisfactory procedures simply because it is afraid to experiment with the new. There can be no effective utilization of trained manpower unless a system is introduced which rewards individuals on the basis of their performance. No private employer would do anything else. No public employer can afford to do otherwise. Employees should know from the day that

they begin work that rewards attach to their doing well
and that penalties are the inevitable consequence of poor
performance.

Another facet of government employment policy which
should be reassessed relates to the hurdles that are presently placed in the path of individuals who seek to shift
from one agency to another. At present, the barriers to
mobility appear to be excessive, especially since individuals who are utilizing their skills effectively are likely to remain where they are. Many of those searching a new job
are likely to be underutilized in their current assignments.
If this is so, their relocation is likely to be of general benefit.

The importance of a career system was discussed at some
considerable length when we considered problems facing
the teaching profession. We will now discuss the feasibility
of approaching many of the government's other personnel
problems in the same terms. Every department of government finds it difficult to fill assignments in outlying posts.
Yet the development of the country requires that many
more professional, technical, and administrative personnel
be assigned to these posts. It will be much easier for government to overcome the present high resistance which
characterizes all trained personnel if it were well understood that assignment to the countryside is not banishment
preparatory to oblivion, but is an initial stage in a series of
gradual moves during which the individual can come
closer to the centers of power and authority in the major
communities.

This chapter has sought to call attention to a few of the
more important points of leverage that can speed the development and utilization of Ethiopia's manpower by
helping to improve the effectiveness with which the educational training, market, and governmental personnel sys-

tems perform their principal missions. The specific recommendations we have advanced are less important than the focus on these several mechanisms and the linkages between the ways in which these mechanisms currently operate and can be made to operate to effect better development and utilization of the nation's manpower.

Many of the problems identified in this chapter and the solutions propounded have relevance to other developing nations. A great many countries in an early stage of industrialization face the challenge of rapidly expanding their educational structure in the face of a qualitative and quantitative shortage of teachers. They too must give high priority to expanding the number of teacher training institutions. But it would be an error to believe that the problem of teacher supply can be solved solely through increasing the output, important as such increases are.

The important point is that the type of training which teachers receive often makes them potentially attractive employees to a great many different sectors of society, including other departments of government itself. Whether they enter or remain in teaching will be determined in large measure by the relative attractions of the profession in comparison to available alternatives. Interestingly, the same excessive concern with the supply of teachers to the neglect of their rewards and utilization which is characteristic of so many developing nations is also present in the manpower planning, or lack thereof, in many advanced economies.

However, many new nations face an additional hurdle. Their people frequently speak different languages and none of the languages has literature adequate for advanced education and training, particularly in scientific and technological fields. Hence one of the Western tongues—usually English or French—becomes an essential tool for those who are preparing themselves for higher level work.

In many developing nations, insufficient attention has been devoted to the difficulties of young people in acquiring knowledge of the dominant language of the country and then gaining mastery of a language that unlocks the knowledge and science of the West. Better language instruction, especially teaching young people how to read a new language, holds the key to raising the effectiveness of many burgeoning school systems. For without early competence in a foreign language, students are not likely to profit much from their secondary, and less from their college, education.

However, it is an error to equate education with literacy as many countries do. Much of the adult population in most of the developing nations is likely to be illiterate. Yet adults, too, need more knowledge if only so they can bring up their children better and understand why they should make special efforts to facilitate their education.

In light of the potential of the transistor radio and other modern techniques of inexpensive communication, too little effort has been devoted to ways of broadening and deepening adult education in many developing nations.

Difficult as are the problems of expanding educational opportunities, many developing nations have compounded them on the one hand by making the life of the college student too attractive and, on the other, by seeking to overcome manpower deficiencies through compulsory devices. While few families can pay anything toward the education of an offspring, even one of great talent, it does not follow that governments which are hard pressed must cover all of the student's expenses—tuition, maintenance, supplies, spending money, and travel allowances—through outright grants. This only intensifies the pressures on those seeking a higher education, many of whom may be at-

tracted more by the prospect of an easy and eventually secure life than by a genuine drive to develop their latent
capacities and later to employ them productively. There is
no reason that the sincerity of the student body should not
be tested through a stipend that is part grant and part
loan. The earnest student will eventually be able to earn
more than enough to repay a loan. The government's limited funds will go further and the seriousness of the educational process will be underscored.

Governments, of course, know of the advantages which
accrue to the favored few whom they have subsidized, but
the usual way in which they have sought to extract a return has been through one or another form of compulsory
service. While such a demand may be proper, especially if
there is no other way to assure that outlying areas can attract teachers and other trained personnel, there are difficulties connected with the use of compulsion. Often bureaucrats seek to solve intractable personnel problems by
increasing their reliance on compulsion. But this deflects
attention from serious drawbacks to the underlying salary
levels and career incentives. If these are seriously awry, as
they frequently are, compulsion will be at best a stopgap
and not always a successful one. The weakness in administrative structures, typical of many developing nations,
places many difficulties in the path of operating a compulsory system effectively and equitably.

What is usually needed—and much to be preferred—is a
careful analysis of the differentials which exist between
teaching and other competitive opportunities and a career
system which goes as far as possible to remove the disadvantages from teaching as a life's work. Such a plan need
not aim at making teaching fully competitive since many
young people who chose teaching want to teach. Nor need
it aim at holding all or even most of those who initially

prepare themselves for teaching in the field. A more reasonable and realistic objective would be to reduce the outflow so that efforts aimed at enlarging the supply would result in reasonable increments.

✦9✦

The Longer View

THE ANALYSIS so far should have answered some of the
questions raised in chapter 1, "What Is a Manpower
Study?" As happens frequently, the negative answers
emerged more sharply than the positive ones. We have
seen that a manpower study does not imply constructing
successive economic development plans from fair, frequently poor, data, and calculating the manpower deriva-
tives from them. The art and science of economic planning
is simply too primitive to justify detailed derivations unless they are undertaken for the purpose of establishing
parameters against which to check a series of alternative
calculations.

It is worth noting in passing that the original economic
plan for Ethiopia inadvertently omitted any consideration
of the expansion of public health, although in point of fact
this particular ministry was later characterized by relatively rapid expansion. We have also noted that there has
been a shortfall of the order of 25 percent in the rate of
expansion in manufacturing from the estimates of the last
plan. Instead of almost 58,000 employees in this sector by
next year, the more likely figure will be 44,000. One addi-

tional point: a careful analysis of the budget and expenditure patterns reveals that it has been difficult on more than one occasion for the government to spend all the money on development projects within the stipulated time period. The unspent funds have usually been transferred to help pay for ordinary operations. This proves that it is frequently easier to allocate sums for development projects on paper than it is to invest money wisely for expansion. Therefore, all manpower plans based on development plans must be treated circumspectly and used only to help sketch the broad outlines, never the details.

But if manpower planning cannot be based on development planning, on what can it be based? There are several ways of responding to this admittedly difficult question. The first is to recognize that all markets, even those characteristic of developing societies, have considerable flexibility. That is another way of saying that current gaps between the demand and supply for trained persons will call forth one or more types of adjustment: importing skilled workers from abroad; attempting to substitute capital for labor and thus reduce the need for certain types of skill; upgrading those who have at least some skills; adjusting wages to draw trained persons out of the areas in which they have been working to those with higher priorities; and reconsidering the qualifications previously demanded for certain types of work which may help to broaden the potential supply of qualified persons.

Each of these approaches has been used and with varying degrees of success in Ethiopia during the past decade. While its experience was not always a happy one, the Imperial Highway Authority relied in considerable measure for its road construction on contractual relations with foreign companies which brought in not only their equipment but also their professional and skilled manpower. In

the most technologically advanced sectors, such as telecommunications, electric power, and airlines, many examples can be found where greater reliance on capital helped
resolve the demand for skills that were in short supply. In
addition, all of the better managed operations in the modern sectors, such as Wonji Sugar, Ethiopian Airlines, and
the several quasi-government corporations (such as Imperial Highways, Telecommunications, the Ethiopian Electric Light and Power Authority) have helped themselves
significantly in overcoming acute skill shortages by insti-
tuting a range of training programs, both in classrooms
and on the job. The role of wage adjustments in the redis-
tribution of trained labor to sectors with priority needs for
skills can be seen in a great many fields—in commercial
activities, in motor vehicle repairs, and in hotel operations.
The adjustment of hiring standards to increase the pool of
potential workers played a major role in the expansion of
the teacher supply, to use that one illustration.

This argument contends that specific manpower planning must be undertaken by those who must get their
missions performed, but given the flexibility that exists in
the market, an overall national plan is not the only way of
balancing manpower supplies and manpower requirements. In the absence of a solid foundation for calculating
skill requirements in detail, national manpower planning,
if carried too far, can lead to more trouble than good.

If these cautionary strictures are justified, how do the
policy-makers obtain guidance so that their development
projects will not founder for lack of skill and, in turn, investments in education and related fields will not result in
many people developing goals that they will be unable to
realize because of a lack of effective demand for their
labor? Manpower planning may be treacherous, but how
can we proceed without it?

The answer to the first query about manpower resources for particular development projects—and for the program as a whole—has already been suggested. Each project must be budgeted out ahead of time, not only in terms of capital requirements and materials but also for skills. When it is clear, as is usually the case in a country in an early stage of modernization, that the market does not have an adequate supply of the required skills, the planning must include provision for importing, training, and upgrading. Only in this manner will the manpower requirements be met. We suggested in the last chapter that the government should pay particular attention to skill development efforts by all contractors, and that it should encourage the full exploitation of all types of training potentialities that currently exist in the country. The government will have to keep some check on prospective requirements and potential output if it pursues this track aggressively. Such a sequential approach to skill aggrandizement is not neat, but we believe that on balance it offers more prospect of success than any alternative type of planning.

The most difficult problem remains. What criteria are to govern the rate of expansion and the direction of the expansion of the educational system? Here, clearly, a policy that is short run and segmented, such as we believe is appropriate in expanding skill, has little or no validity. There is too much evidence in too many developing countries of an educational system which has grown out of balance with the society, the economy, and the fiscal capabilities of government.

We have argued and we iterate here that the factors which should be considered in planning the expansion of the educational system should be sensitive to the manpower scene, but should not be primarily conditioned by it. Some simple facts can help to make this clear. Accord-

ing to the calculations presented in chapter 2, it is highly
likely that three-quarters of the Ethiopian labor force will
still be engaged in agriculture in the year 2000. The probability is that the proportion will be even higher. Therefore any significant expansion of the educational system
must be fundamentally related to the rural population. It
is not a question of its relationship to a population in
which the majority will have a highly diversified occupational distribution. This goes a long way to simplifying the
underlying problems that are involved.

Before looking more closely at the rural population, let
us stipulate why the modern sector—and particularly manufacturing—cannot grow at a rapid rate. The lag between
expectations and accomplishments that has dogged most
developing countries since the end of World War II
derives from a failure to deal with elementary facts. This
has resulted from an admixture of economic naïveté on
the part of the leadership of developing nations and the
pseudo-sophistication of development economists who mis-
took their own paper calculations for realistic accomplishments.

A simple exercise in arithmetic will help to clarify the
situation as far as the prospective industrialization of Ethiopia is concerned. Suppose we set as a forty-year goal that
the economy has 10 percent of its employed population in
manufacturing. Forty years hence, Ethiopia will have a
labor force of at least 15 million; 10 percent implies 1.5
million manufacturing employees. A labor force of which
10 percent is in manufacturing reflects a very modest industrialization. Israel today has almost 20 percent of its
labor force in manufacturing and at that has only an
embryonic manufacturing sector.

If we stipulate that each new manufacturing job in the
modern sector requires about E$15,000 of direct capital

investment—a low figure in terms of the experience of other countries—then for each increment of 100,000 people, there would be a capital requirement of E$1.5 billion. For 15 such increments the requirement would approximate E$22.5 billion. It is probably conservative to postulate that a sum equal to the amount of direct investment would be required for infrastructure. Hence the establishment of 1.5 million manufacturing jobs over a period of forty years would involve a capital investment of about E$1 billion annually or roughly 40 percent of the current Gross National Product.

It is difficult to see how the foregoing calculations are anything but conservative given the paucity of infrastructure that currently prevails. But the estimates are important as regards the orders of magnitude which they suggest. They should make unequivocally clear the reasons for postulating that, under the most favorable of circumstances, at the beginning of the twenty-first century and probably for long thereafter, most Ethiopians will still be engaged in agriculture.

What implications for educational programing can be derived from this fact? Several alternatives are suggested. One would be to keep investment in education in the rural areas as low as possible because there is little prospect that it will be translated into significant productivity gains in the foreseeable future. A second possibility is opposite and argues that the shape of the occupational structure is irrelevant for determining the quantity and quality of an educational effort: it has relevance only for considerations of emphasis within the curriculum.

A third would be that the critical factor in determining the rate at which education should be provided for the rural population is the desire of the people for education and their willingness to contribute by labor and money to its support. In this third approach an estimate must be made whether the anticipations underlying a strong demand for education have some prospect of being fulfilled so that satisfaction rather than frustration will result from an enlarged investment. We have already stipulated that a considerable and probably growing proportion of the rural population is evincing a desire for education and that there is evidence of their willingness to help with the capital requirement and even the operating costs. So far the assessment points in the direction of a positive response.

What is the likelihood, however, with regard to the people who now are clamoring for schools as well as those who will join in the clamor when more schools are erected in their region, that the aspirations currently attached to education will not be fulfilled and that disappointment and hostility will develop? This issue is basic and must be confronted. If most rural people see education as the road to the city, to white-collar employment, to higher incomes, and to a life of ease and excitement, they will not only be disappointed but they will be thoroughly disillusioned. Such prospects will have reality for a small part of the population, surely not for the majority, not even for a significant minority. Therefore the expansion of education must be predicated on other premises and must be interpreted and implemented accordingly. Then, and only then, can it be a positive force.

We have established that the rate of industrialization is likely to be very modest, primarily because of the large amounts of capital that are required to shift a significant minority of a growing labor force into manufacturing. It follows that, in the absence of the discovery of mineral wealth, the growth of per capita income will be quite modest. Within this context, what can be said about the relations of education to agricultural advance, particularly to improvements in the terms of rural life? A great deal can be stipulated about the strategic opportunities for education to bring about major gains in the well-being of the Ethiopian population by dynamizing the terms of rural life. Unless the farmer changes, Ethiopia will not change very much. And for the farmer to change, something new and important must be introduced into his culture. This new element can only be education. No other force has the potentiality of so large an impact.

Whether and to what degree the heavily populated farm lands of the north and the virgin and sparsely settled farm land of the south can be cultivated so as to yield much more than currently will depend on a great many different factors, including more expert knowledge about the inherent qualities of the soil and the best ways of cultivating the land. We have noted that significant changes in agriculture will require new infrastructure, such as roads and dams, the eradication of malaria, new capital inputs in the form of fertilizer, improved seed and stock, and machinery. But in addition to these difficult and costly resource transformations, an improved agriculture will require a new outlook on the part of the farm population together with the rapid diffusion and application of new knowledge among them so that they will be able to get a larger return from their own labor and from such resources as they control. Education alone will not be able to alter significantly the productivity of Ethiopian agriculture, but it is impossible to see how agriculture can be altered unless individual farmers develop a new view of life and work. And if this is to happen then education—on a broad scale—appears to be the *sine qua non*.

There are values in addition to a rise in agricultural productivity that can be anticipated from a rapid penetration of education into the countryside. The quality of the

farmer's life is greatly affected at the present time by disease, premature death, irrational beliefs and patterns of
behavior, hopelessness—to mention only these. Once again,
education alone will not be sufficient to eliminate the
many sources of infectious, contagious, nutritional, and
other diseases, but it could surely make a significant contribution to raising the levels of personal hygiene; it could
improve eating habits and contribute to communal sanitation. If it did these things—and if the population did not
increase at an accelerating rate, the terms of life in the
rural areas could be significantly improved, even though
per capita income as it is customarily measured would
show only modest gains.

There is still another front along which rural education
could make a substantial contribution. We have noted that
a high proportion of the rural population suffers from
underemployment in addition to unemployment. Labor
which is not used means that goods and services are not
produced which could have enriched the members of the
community. There is no assurance that education will enable people to alter their conventional practices so as to
put the labor which has been running to waste to constructive use. But it holds the promise of making such a change
possible. If it succeeds along these lines even partially, it
will yield high social dividends.

The potentialities for such a constructive impact are
somewhat greater because of the pioneering efforts of the
Ethiopian government to push community development
projects and training. The Ministry of Community Development has set up twenty-two community development
centers, one or more in each of the major provinces. All
of the centers, except the one in Asmara, are village centers. The concept is to tie together into a comprehensive
program education, health services, sanitation and water

supply, market organization, agricultural productivity, and road improvements. The organizational frame has been for a center to encompass a rural population of about 20,000 inhabitants. Each center has a development officer with ten multipurpose technicians. To assist in the training of specialized personnel a school was opened at Awassa in July, 1960. Students are tapped off at the eleventh and twelfth grades, and the course of study is one year. The annual output has been fluctuating between 60 and 80. As one might suspect the difficulties involved in launching such a pioneering effort are many and they are only slowly being brought under control.

There remain several potent arguments in favor of the expansion of education into the countryside just as rapidly as scarce resources of money and teachers permit. Education is the only innovation that holds the promise of providing a window to the better future that all people now know is possible and even consider their right. A government that is oblivious to the strength of this desire will not only cause disappointment and suffering to the awakening masses but will jeopardize its own future. For no people will be denied for long.

Reference was made earlier to the fact that it has not always been possible for the Ethiopian government to spend the money it had allocated for specific development projects. An educational expansion program provides an excellent opportunity to absorb available funds. There are of course many fields where large sums can be invested if the matter of short-run returns is waived. But are there in fact so many projects for which the people realize that the expenditures are made directly on their behalf? A new dam or a new road may be attractive, but dollar for dollar a great many more poeple can receive a valuable benefit through expenditures on education. Of course, these ex-

penditures must be the foundation for constructive reforms. As we have argued earlier, unless education is able
to better the terms of rural life, it will have failed.

Some indication of the scope of education as a field of
potential investment is suggested by the following data. At
present, with 350,000 children in grades one through six
out of a total of 3.7 million between the ages of 7 to 12,
approximately 9.4 percent of the cohort is currently in
school. But this is a national average. The range is from 56
percent in Addis Ababa and 27 percent in Eritrea to 4.3
percent in Goma Gofa, 3.5 percent in Harar, and 3 percent
in Wallo. There are four other provinces that fall below
the national norm: Tigre, Gojjan, Arussi, and Sidamo.
Clearly there is great scope for expansion at the elementary level.

The parallel figures for junior high school—grades seven
and eight and corresponding to ages 13 and 14—show a
total of about 25,000 students out of slightly under 1
million in the cohort, or a ratio of 2.5 percent for the nation as a whole. The ratio of all the provinces except
Eritrea and Shoa fall far below the national average, which
indicates the heavy concentration of junior high schools in
the principal cities.

The figures covering grades nine through twelve and the
age group 15 to 19 shows the same general distribution as
among the junior high-school population. With 23,000 high-
school students out of an age population of about 1.6 million, the ratio for the nation as a while stands at 1.5 percent. Once again, all of the provinces other than Eritrea
and Shoa fall below, most of them considerably below, the
national norm. The scope for additional investment in education, particularly rural education, is very large indeed.

A few additional observations about the significance of a
rapid expansion of rural education. We have pointed out

that there is little chance of moving Ethiopia ahead unless the agricultural hinterland begins to move. And it will be next to impossible to introduce significant orders of change in the hinterland unless advantage is taken of the interest and concern of the population in education. Of course, effective penetration cannot rely on education alone. Unless roads are built and ties established between outlying areas and neighboring towns, it will be impossible to attract and retain teachers in the deeper recesses of the country. But if these and other hurdles are ovecome, education is probably the most potent force for penetrating the countryside.

One of the major difficulties that many developing countries have experienced as a result of their concentrating on industrialization and urbanization has been that the city is set up as a powerful magnet that has drawn large numbers of rural people, particularly poorly educated rural youth, into the urban centers where they have not been readily absorbed. While Ethiopia has not been free of this problem, at least as far as Addia Ababa and Asmara are concerned, this situation is still relatively under control. One of the significant gains that can be contemplated from the proposal to expand rural education rapidly, with an aim of improving the conditions of rural life, is the possibility of avoiding an excessive flow of country people into the city. It is assumed that as education expands, rural life will improve. On this basis there is ground for cautious optimism about the possibility of maintaining a reasonable rural-urban balance.

This much appears clear from the experiences of other African nations. The failure of government to concern itself with the countryside can produce tremendous problems in a very short time. We have no ready answer to how to handle the unemployment of rural youth who are now

in the larger cities other than to recommend efforts to put
them to work at the same time that an effort is made to increase their skills. But government must move cautiously
here, else through its own actions it will set up a stronger
flow. Its major long-range efforts must be directed to improving conditions in the countryside so that the numbers
seeking to flee are held to a reasonable level.

Effective development policies and progress require that
the tendency for generations to be estranged from each other
be mitigated rather than intensified. Despite its enthusi-
asms and its energies, youth alone cannot make over a society. Another important gain, therefore, from a long-
range rural improvement program, is the prospect of
educating the younger generation while helping to change
the attitudes and behavior of the older generation. The
more this is done, the greater the momentum for change.

Closely related is the importance of opening opportunities not only for boys and men but also for girls and
women. One of the barriers to development in most un-
derdeveloped societies are rigid sex lines. If education
begins to unsettle the established structure, it may make a
significant contribution to development. This much is
clear: since improvements in the terms of rural life require
changes in health, sanitation, and diet, the cooperation of
women must be secured.

A country cannot be developed except by its own people. A government can lead the way. Foreign experts can
help. But little will transpire unless the mass of the population eventually gets caught up in the process. They must
want to change; they must be willing to make the effort to
change; and they must in considerable measure provide
the resources required to effectuate changes. This explains
why in countries where most of the people live at or close
to subsistence, development is so illusive. But a sound

strategy recognizes the problem and seeks to solve it in an appropriate manner. To speed the development of an overwhelmingly agricultural people, one must seek to change the ways of life of the farm population.

This lesson of the predominant importance of planning for agriculture is slowly being learned by both those responsible for shaping the policies and programs of developing nations and the advisers from more advanced economies who work along side of them. It has taken many years, large sums, and the accumulation of a host of difficult if not intractable problems before many of the planners were able to realize that industrialization and urbanization are not an "open sesame" to progress.

Cities have always acted as magnets which draw country people off the farm in search of excitement and the better life. But if the flow into the urban center is greatly in excess of the jobs that are opening up—as has in fact been the case in many parts of Latin America, Africa, and Asia —potential explosions rather than social progress looms ahead.

This presents one more cogent reason to improve the conditions of rural life—to prevent the flooding of the cities with unabsorbable hordes of farmers and farmers' children. Therefore, one imperative is to relate the education that is provided the rural population to the problems and prospects which they face in their own locales. It is essential to develop curricula that will provide most students with the opportunity of putting to use what they have learned in a way that will contribute to raising their economic well-being and their terms of life. Rural education must be related to improving health, increasing agricultural productivity, and broadening recreational and social activities. Otherwise, it may only make a primarily stable population disgruntled, and its young people may

wander off to the city where they will be unable to sink
roots and will therefore remain suspended between their
old world and the new.

Concern that education may unsettle the status quo does
not mean that the government should ignore the latent
and expressed demand of the agricultural population for
schools for their children. There are fewer and fewer
places in the world where the drive for education has not
yet penetrated into the most outlying areas.

A wise government will not ignore this pressure but will
seek to channel it. There is increasing evidence from many
developing countries that the population is so avid for
educational opportunity for their children that they will
do a great deal to help bring it about. Government should
therefore encourage the local population to contribute as
much as they can both to the building of the school and to
its operation. Not only will local contributions ease the
strain on tight governmental budgets but they will provide
a new focus for communal action at the local level. And
one of the principal aims of development must be to introduce and take advantage of forces which may indeed
unsettle the status quo but which can be successfully chan-
neled to a constructive end.

✦ 10 ✦

The Next Steps

NO MATTER how much time, effort, and resources are devoted to a manpower study, it is inherent in the nature of development that an inquiry undertaken at one
point in time will have a relatively short life. It can provide direction for the years immediately ahead and, if it
does its task well, it will highlight important areas where
definitive conclusions must be postponed because of lack
of data. And it will call attention to certain dynamic forces
which are altering important parameters of the manpower
problem. The more substantial the study, the more certain
that it will forecast its own short life by pointing out how
new data and new developments will require reappraisals
and reassessments of manpower policy and programing.

In a country such as Ethiopia, which has never had a
census, where the educational system is just beginning to
penetrate the countryside where most of the population
lives, where relatively little information is available about
the changing role of foreigners in the economy beyond the
generally accepted belief that they dominate the modern
sector, where the government has been the principal employer of trained manpower but may now be reaching a

limit with respect to adding many more to its administrative payroll, where, for security reasons, almost no information is available about skill development in the Armed Forces or about its impingement on the civilian sector, where the scope and scale of assistance from abroad remains subject to substantial uncertainty—in the face of these many unknowns it must be clear that no study can be more than a link in an ongoing chain. Ethiopia needs a continuing effort at data collection and analysis, not a one-time set of conclusions. For no matter how valid the conclusions may be at the time they are advanced, they will inevitably be subject to major correction and change as new and better data become available and as various trends are interrupted or even reversed, while others become important.

The principal aim of this concluding chapter is to set forth in brief context the goals, structure, and administration of manpower studies in a developing country such as Ethiopia. An effort will be made to delineate a realistic plan which is sensitive to the limitations of technical and other resources rather than an ideal approach. In fact, the scale of a manpower effort cannot be determined in advance, since it will depend on a great many factors, including the rate at which reliable data are accumulated, analyzed, and utilized.

What should be the interim goals of a newly launched effort at manpower analysis? A first effort must be directed to broadening and deepening the factual information about the nation's manpower resources. Primary attention should be devoted to learning more about the supply of trained persons, both those currently employed as well as those in the preparatory stream. Since we noted repeatedly the differences which exist between the larger and smaller cities and between the urban and rural areas, a knowledge of gross totals can only be a starting point, not an end point, in any thorough analysis of manpower. Policy-makers need to know not only the size and changes in the totals, but detailed information which will reveal how the limited numbers of trained persons are distributed throughout the country, and, equally important, the contributions of different regions to the new supply.

Although most jobs outside the self-sufficient economy of the countryside have long been held by males, it would be an error to perpetuate this practice and pay scant regard to females. Women have begun to play an increasingly important role in selected sectors of the modern economy. Moreover, women in the cities, who have greater access to education, will represent a potentially valuable supply of individuals who, through additional education and training, can be added to the limited numbers of trained personnel. Therefore, a study of manpower resources must differentiate by sex as well as by region.

Although developing countries are frequently handicapped by insufficient data of indifferent quality, effective manpower research is not dependent upon the accumulation of ever larger bodies of information. Many highly developed countries are inundated by materials, but they have not clearly delineated the facts and figures required for sound policy formulation. It is important for a country such as Ethiopia to avoid this problem. Ethiopia needs to improve its basic educational data—that is, information about the flow of students passing through the successive levels of the school system, the repeaters, the drop-outs, the numbers who pass and fail various important examinations, and other measures which would help to provide knowledge not only about the numbers who are being educated but also the quality of education which they are receiving.

To understand the structure and operation of this critically important part of the manpower shaping institutions, the educational data should be expanded to reflect more about the teacher supply, not only the size of the different subgroups of teachers—elementary, junior and senior high school—but their important characteristics, their level of formal education, their age, their length of time in the profession, national and ethnic backgrounds, and other relevant characteristics that will illuminate not only the quantity but also the quality of the teacher supply. Just as information about drop-outs among students is important, so is information about the mobility and turnover of teachers.

A related though much more difficult task will be the systematic collection of data about ancillary training institutions, their staffs, and student flows. Developing countries cannot afford to repeat the errors made by developed countries of focusing their manpower planning almost exclusively on the formal educational structure. Certainly schools play a critical role in manpower development. But so do many institutions outside of the formal educational system. We have emphasized repeatedly the role that various specialized training institutions in Ethiopia have played in enlarging the pool of middle-level skills and the significant proportion of the country's talent pool that was tapped off for such specialized instruction. We suggested that the flow into and through these specialized institutions is likely to increase still further. Therefore, it is important to collect reliable data about these operations.

It is important to pay some attention to the still less formally structured efforts at skill development that take place through on-the-job training. We have noted that certain organizations, such as the Ethiopian Airlines and the Imperial Highway Authority, engage in large-scale efforts at training and upgrading of their work force. We also observed that in a market economy it is inevitable that some significant proportion of those who are trained in one environment will find their way into other jobs, usually in response to better opportunities which have become open to them as a result of their training. An attempt to inventory the numbers in the nation's skill-pool must count the contributions made by on-the-job training and by what, for lack of a better term, can be defined as pick-up skills, where men on their own succeed in adding to their knowledge and competence by informal or formal study, by changing jobs, and by other ways.

Once the educational-training structure has been delineated and the basic data in each of the appropriate cells refined, a foundation will have been established for a framework within which to make various estimates about the future supplies of trained persons. Without a reliable base, future estimates will have little validity. Even with good data about the past and present, estimates of the future may still be awry. But the probability of their validity is greater if the estimator starts from a sound base.

Much more difficult—yet equally if not more important —are studies of the future demand for trained manpower. Here we confront problems that no country, not even one with a controlled economy and using econometric models and advanced computers, has been able to surmount successfully. The future demand for skilled manpower is a function of the overall rate of economic development, the composition of future output, and the use of complementary and competing resources.

In a country such as Ethiopia, where considerable scope remains to the individual entrepreneur to determine whether to invest and in what to invest, and where the government's access to development funds is not predetermined and its use of available funds also remains open, it is not possible to do more than make a range of estimates about the future level of the economy and to derive therefrom the manpower dimensions.

There is the further uncertainty which may result from changes in the manner of production. Because of likely changes in manpower supplies, the cost of capital, and improvements in technology, the existing ratios among trained and untrained manpower and capital are likely to be altered.

One rule about the future demand for manpower: If the period covered by the estimate is short, the possibility of error is less. In addition, a more general forecast is less likely to contain error. A calculation about the future demand for engineers is likely to be better than a forecast of the demand for mechanical engineers.

The embryonic manpower specialist must learn about the difficulties in calculating future demand and the ways he can hedge his bets. The sophisticated analyst understands the critically important element of substitutability. He learns that without the required numbers of fully trained professionals, employers are likely to improvise and use a larger number of technicians.

The important role of foreigners in Ethiopia is another balancing wheel. If the demand for trained manpower turns out to be in excess of the available supply, more reliance is likely to be placed on foreigners. If matters go the other way, foreigners are likely to be discouraged from entering or remaining in employment. The problems connected with estimating manpower demand can be understood only by making the attempt and checking out one's forecasts over time, identifying as well as possible the factors responsible for the correctness or errors in the forecasts.

Manpower specialists play an important role in the development of the art of manpower analysis. Since these specialists can never be fully trained within an academic setting, let us consider briefly the types of persons who are likely to do well in this new and still only partially structured discipline. Certainly people with different types of education can do equally well in the manpower field, subject only to their having an interest in the processes of human development and a basic sense of quantitative and qualitative relationships. While a flair for numbers is essential for competence in manpower analysis, training in advanced mathematics or statistics is not a prerequisite nor even necessarily a desideratum. The judgments which are required must be grounded more in a sense of history and institutions and the market place than in deductions from axioms. Since manpower analysis deals with a strategic resource, and since the discipline of economics centers on the study of the allocation of scarce resources and their utilization, training in economics is a good route into the manpower field.

In addition to a sense of numbers and training in economics, a sensitivity for the cultural, social, and psychological factors that influence the way in which individuals and groups see themselves and their future in relation to the barriers and opportunities in the larger society is important. Thus, if the manpower analyst is to be effective, he must be broadly trained; he must prefer the field of political economy in which many axes intersect to the mathematical model-building of the econometrician.

Since the university is graduating a considerable number of young people who have majored in economics with a minor in statistics, and since graduates in other fields frequently have the prerequisites for doing good work in manpower analysis, material from which manpower specialists can be drawn is available. The question is how the young person can acquire a higher order of competence and sophistication in a relatively short time.

One answer is a conducive and supportive environment. We have been impressed that the Central Statistical Office is making sound progress both in the collection of basic demographic data and in their analyses. Therefore, the apprenticeship of young men with an interest in manpower to the Central Statistical Office has much to commend it.

Even though we have been exceedingly cautious in translating planning documents into manpower terms, we recognize the importance of the Planning Board as an instrument of government policy and the links between its work and manpower analysis. Therefore, to attach one or more young men with an interest in manpower to the Planning Board may be desirable.

Since the present government reorganization provides for a new Ministry of Economic Development, which will incorporate both the Central Statistical Office and the Planning Board with other units, and since development planning should be infused with manpower considerations since it will have a major impact on manpower plans, there is overriding reason for several young men with a primary concern with manpower problems to be attached to this new ministry.

Another basic relationship is between manpower and education. Much of this report was focused on the analysis of the supply of trained manpower and the role of the educational system. Effective manpower analysis requires, therefore, a close link with the Ministry of Education.

The two major outposts for manpower planning are the Ministry of Economic Development and the Ministry of Education. Where is the proper locale for the central effort? In our opinion, the Ethiopian government made a logical decision when it placed the new manpower effort within the Ministry of National Community Development. Its title notwithstanding, this ministry includes what in Western terminology is usually defined as the Department of Labor. And the closest links both in theory and practice are, or should be, between manpower and labor.

Because of the difficulties of collecting basic data, and the possibility of correcting these limitations only slowly, we believe that it would be desirable to place one or more members of the central group of manpower analysts with the key ministries of Economic Development and Education, where they will be close to the problems of basic data collection and analysis. We believe that analysts can often do better work if they are close to the basic sources of information. Not everybody need be at the source, but some must be there.

The successful operation of a manpower resources division, with some of its personnel on detached service with these two ministries and others working out of the central unit within the Ministry of National Community Development, will hinge primarily on the administrative and professional leadership of the central unit. Young people with good potential will develop only if they are properly trained. The only person who can train them is their supervisor. A first challenge therefore in establishing a truly effective manpower resource division is to find a strong man to head it.

Because manpower planning and analysis is a relatively new discipline, and because the university is restricted to the instruction of undergraduates, we believe that it would be desirable for the chief of the division, as well as some of the junior personnel, to spend varying periods of time abroad to acquire knowledge of theory, approaches, and techniques which they will be unable to acquire at home. However, since a new unit cannot get started unless some of the staff is engaged in inquiries and analyses, a balance will have to be reached between those on working assignments and those who are studying abroad. We feel no more than two persons should be abroad at one time, and their period of foreign study should not exceed one year, and possibly less. Nobody should be sent abroad in this connection until he has demonstrated the ability and general orientation that foreshadows his capacity to do good work in the manpower field.

If the Ethiopian government were able to allocate eight to ten professional positions to the manpower unit for work throughout the ministries, it would be highly efficient to obtain the services of a competent foreign expert to provide a year of in-service training to the Ethiopian staff. There is much to be said for training a staff in the environment within which it must carry on its work. If the government were to make a firm commitment to strengthen manpower analysis, it would be easier to obtain the services of a foreign expert.

In connection with our study, the government established, under the Minister of National Community Development, a National Manpower Advisory Committee with representatives from each of the key ministries and from major nongovernmental bodies, such as the Haile Selassie I University and the Employers Association. The deliberations of this committee contributed substantially to shaping the nature of the present inquiry and served as a sounding board for a review of preliminary findings.

With such a strong start, there are good reasons to anticipate that the committee can continue to play a major role in the development of manpower policy in Ethiopia. The fact that so many different government departments are represented on the committee establishes the first pre-requisite for the improved collection and evaluation of the basic data. A sound foundation for cooperative action has been laid.

To strengthen this foundation, we recomend that the Manpower Resources Division be placed in the Office of the Minister of National Community Development so that it will have the status that it requires to work effectively across ministerial lines. We also believe that an able and interested official with professional and administrative competence should be placed in charge of the division. The several tasks to which he must direct himself—to secure, train, and upgrade his staff, to design effective research programs, to develop and maintain liasion with other governmental and nongovernmental agencies, to serve as Secretariat for the National Manpower Advisory Committee, and to prepare documents for the guidance of government and for publication—represent a range of duties and responsibilities that can be carried out successfully only by a highly competent civil servant. If the Ethiopian government can appoint a competent man for this assignment, it has reason, particularly because of the demonstrated value of the National Manpower Advisory Committee and the embryonic staff, to look ahead to a steady growth in its manpower program.

Although the membership of the National Manpower Advisory Committee correctly includes both governmental and nongovernmental personnel, major nongovernmental agencies such as the university, the Employers Association, and the trade unions, must initiate and carry out manpower studies and research under their own aegis. Each of these organizations, as well as others in the private sector, has a deep and continuing concern with such basic questions as the prospective supplies of and demand for differ-

ent groups of professional, technical, and skilled manpower. They must be concerned about such matters as pay,
working conditions, and utilization. Moreover, they cannot ignore problems connected with the expansion of their
operations. Thus there are many manpower problems in
which they have a direct and continuing interest. Therefore, they must direct such resources as they can to the systematic analysis of manpower problems that are of direct
concern to them. The results of their inquiries and assess-
ments can be added to those obtained by government and
improved information and sounder conclusions will
emerge.

The university, for both its own guidance and the
guidance of the nation as a whole, must find an early opportunity to establish on-going research in the manpower
field. Even though Ethiopia is at an early stage of development and has a limited number of competent research personnel, it would be an error to have a single focus for manpower research, and that within government. The governmental effort must be the major one, since the basic
information derives primarily from governmental operations in such diverse fields as education, economic development, and agriculture. But a nation that wants to keep
perspective and balance on such crucial matters as the
development and utilization of its manpower resources
must not rely upon a single agency for guidance. Multiple
sources of research provide some insurance against bias and
prejudice. The effectiveness of the National Manpower
Advisory Committee will be greater if it has the benefit of
both governmental and nongovernmental research to guide
its deliberations.

It took the United States 179 years before the Congress
established the framework for a national manpower policy,

including support for research and an advisory committee structure. Ethiopia has moved expeditiously to recognize the challenge and to respond to it. The present study is a link in a chain. A broad dissemination of the results of this study and a critical appraisal of its findings and recommendations will represent another significant advance. If the government also acts on the recommendations advanced above to establish a strong Manpower Resources Division in the Office of the Minister of National Community Development, and if care is taken to build on the excellent beginnings of the National Manpower Advisory Committee, Ethiopia will be in a strong position to develop sound manpower policies. A sound mechanism for manpower policy determination can make a significant and on-going contribution to economic development and, more importantly, to improving the quality of life of the entire citizenry. This is the opportunity that Ethiopia now faces.

Developing countries have paid a high price in mistaken attempts to duplicate, frequently without adaptation, the most advanced approaches and techniques in use in advanced technological societies. This applies to their investment programs where they have frequently put entirely too high a proportion of scarce funds in costly capital equipment while faced with intractable problems of creating more jobs for their unemployed and underemployed population. And it also characterizes much of their planning and administrative structuring where they have likewise sought to imitate countries much further ahead in industrialization.

It is not invidious or demeaning to point out that a nation's planning and administrative structure should be geared to the problems which it confronts, the data which it has available, and the manpower and other resources that it can assign to the planning function. Within these strictures there are a few errors that should be avoided, a few opportunities that should not be missed.

It is an error for developing countries to place much faith on sophisticated models which require a large amount and a good quality of data. For most developing nations have poor data—poor both in quantity and quality.

In addition if their efforts at development are to be reasonably successful, there will be many discontinuities from one time period to another. This means that the data and the relationships prevailing in the past will not be reliable guides to the future. Developing countries need analysts who are knowledgeable about what has happened and why it has happened, but who will also be sensitive to how things may be different in the future. This is particularly important with reference to new policies and new programs that are under way or about to be launched.

For manpower studies, therefore, the aim should be to attract a small but able group of people who have the basic educational prerequisites for work on manpower problems to create the conditions within the governmental structure where they can be closely associated with two centers—that where basic data are assembled and evaluated and that where basic economic programs are initiated and implemented. The manpower analysts need to be close to both. They then will be able to broaden and deepen their own competence by exposure and experience, and they will soon be able to make a reciprocal contribution by suggesting important facets about manpower that are significant for both the data collecting and the programing groups. In this way the economic planners, the census statisticians, and the manpower analysts can reinforce each other with important spill-offs for such major sectors as education, the armed services, and many others.

One other point remains. While in a developing country the center of decision-making and analysis with regard to manpower, as in many other regards, must remain in government, it is essential that govenment does not act alone in manpower policy and programing. Manpower policy involves the vital interests of the individual, voluntary groups, and other nongovernmental bodies. Hence a manpower strategy for a developing as well as for a developed country should be so structured as to provide a place for each sector to play a role. Only then can the latent strengths of all be successfully tapped and utilized.

Index

Agriculture: output, 14, 15, 25, 26 (*tab*), 113, 159–60; labor force in, 24, 74, 88, 156; training schools, 83; demand for trained manpower, 83–84, 87; problems in, 84; reforms, 87; Alemaya graduates in, 102; rural life and productivity, 113, 159–60; two-year diploma course for technicians, 117

Alemaya College, 18; occupations of graduates, 101–2; recommendations on, 117

Apprenticeship system, 145

Bonding system, 138–40
Building College in Addis Ababa, 18

Central Statistical Office, 174
Church schools, 113–14
Civil Service: importance as employer, 33–34, 35, 71, 73, 76–79, 88; trained manpower employed in, 37, 76–79, 86–87; selectivity in college-graduate hiring, 77, 78–79; changes in nature of demand, 86–87; authority delegation in, 92; utilization of skills in, 92–93; mobility in, 92–93, 147; hiring standards, 94; salaries in, 98, 99; personnel policy needs, 108; employment policy, 146–47; merit system in, 146–47; career system in, 147

College graduates: foreign study by, 18, 19, 102–5, 144; salaries of, 40, 77, 91, 142; government demand for, 76–79; government selectivity in hiring, 77, 78–79; cost of government hiring, 78; utilization in Civil Service, 92–93; controlling number of, 119–20, 121, 130–31, 132

Community development projects for rural areas, 77–78, 160–61, 166
Construction industry, 71, 73
Coptic Church, 16

Economic growth, 24–25, 26 (*tab*), 70; literacy and, 12; foreign assistance and, 19–20; projected, 74, 156–58; government in stimulation, 75; in private sector, 75–76, 86; demand and, 88; education and, 109–10; per capita income increases, 158

Economic planning, 3, 84–86, 152; implementation time, 2–3; manpower planning and, 84–86, 153; elementary education expansion and, 111–16; rural life improvement and, 112–13, 164–66; relat-

Economic planning (*Continued*)
ing educational system to, 130–31,
132; skill requirements and, 155;
gearing to real problems, 179–80
Education: skill acquisition and, 9,
69; language problems and, 13–
14, 111, 115, 136, 148–51; foreign,
18, 19, 102–5, 144; in rural areas,
23; school attendance and community size, 32–33; quality, 33,
130, 131–32; commitments and incentives for, 40–41, 137–39, 141,
149–50; enrollment in schools, 47–
52, 162; of physicians, 80–81, 82;
of nurses, 81–82; of agricultural
specialists, 83–84; wage-gearing
to, 91, 145–46; of foreign population, 96, 97; utilization problem
in, 100–1; competence related to,
107; church schools in, 113–14;
curriculum guidelines, 114–16,
117, 119, 120–21, 132; extension
program in, 118–19; role and capacities, 122–23; aims of, 129–31,
132; aids for teachers, 136–37; of
nonliterate, 137, 149; rural life
changes and, 159–61, 163–66; improvement of data on, 169–70; for
manpower analysis, 173–74
Educational system: government
and, 17–18, 34; foreign aid for,
18–19, 51; financing, 18–19, 20, 51,
67, 123–26, 131; capacity, 36; problems in expansion, 37, 46, 67, 111–
19, 126–29, 148; relating to manpower planning, 43, 114–16, 119–
22, 130–31, 132, 157; foreign prototype use, 67–69, 129–30; economic development and, 73, 109–10;
administration-teacher   conflicts,
100, 101; cost of expansion, 112–
13; teacher shortage and, 126–29;
goals of, 129–31; control of student flow through, 132; criteria
for expansion, 134–36, 155–58;
recommendations on, 140–43; as
field for potential investment,
161–62
Elementary schools: preparation

level of teachers, 62–63; importance of expansion, 111–19; per
capita pupil costs in, 125; available teacher supply for, 126; projected need for teachers, 127, 128–
29; enrollment in, 162
Enrollment in schools, 47–52; secondary schools, 53–54, 162; university, by faculty, 58–59; university, by grade, 58–60; university
policies on, 66, 116–17, 119–20,
121, 132; in extension programs,
118–19; teacher shortage and projected, 127–28; elementary schools,
162
Eritrea, 17
Ethiopian Airlines, 18, 35, 94–95,
170–71
Ethiopian Electric Light and Power
Authority, 95
Ethiopian School Leaving Certificate (ESLC), 41; proportion of
students passing, 52–53, 60; validity in screening, 53
Ethiopian University Service, 64,
128, 138
Extension programs in education,
118–19

Foreign assistance, 18–20, 29
Foreigners: employment of, as indication of supply-demand, 7,
172; occupations of, 16, 96, 97; as
trained manpower source, 19, 36,
153–54; relations with local work
force, 39–40; natives vs., in responsible positions, 43; as teachers, 62–66, 100, 128, 135; utilization in private sector, 94; population parameters, 95–96; work permits for, 96; education of, 96, 97;
salaries of, 96–97; policy for replacement, 107–8; role in training system, 144–45
Foreign study, 18, 19, 102–5, 144

Government: strengthening, 17; investment and economic development, 34–35; modernization and

efficiency of, 35–36; manpower utilization regulations, 41–42, 137–39, 141, 149–50; in stimulation of economic growth, 75; decentralization plans, 77–78

Government expenditures, 25; financing, 28–29; growth of, 28, 35, 86–87; on military, 34; demand for trained manpower and, 35, 86–87, 88; policies on educational, 67, 131; on health, 82; limitations on, 83; on education, 109–10, 112–13, 123–26; funds available for educational, 123–24; per capita student costs, 125; recommendations on educational, 134–36; development planning fund surplus, 153, 161–62; scope of educational field for, 161–62

Government revenues: increases in, 28, 86; available for education, 123–24, 126, 131

Haile Selassie I, Emperor, 13, 17–18
Haile Selassie I University, 19, 58–61, 64–66, 80–83; see also University
Handicrafts, 71
Health problems, 15, 79–80, 82, 83, 160
Health services, 73; rural program, 17–18; rural vs. urban areas, 33; government role in, 34; demand for trained manpower in, 79–83; government expenditures on, 82; expansion of, 152

Illiteracy, 13, 22–23; economic expansion and, 12; prospects for decline, 23; community size and, 32–33; education in elimination, 137, 149
Imperial Highway Authority, 94, 95, 153, 170–71
Industrialization: of developing nations, 45–46; demand and, 88; projected rate, 156–58; urbanization and, 163, 165
In-service training programs, 55–58,

94–95; as supply-demand indication, 7; private vs. government, 94; skill shortages and, 154, 170–71
International Bank for Reconstruction and Development, 29, 34
International Development Agency, 29, 51
Investment: possibilities in, 3–4, 75–76, 171–72; government vs. private, 34–35, 36; required for industrial expansion, 156–57
Italian occupation, 17

Labor force, 23–24; occupational distribution, 24, 88; estimated nonagricultural, 71–73, 74; in agriculture, 74, 88, 156; in manufacturing, 88, 152–53
Land: tenure systems, 14–15; population ratio to, 15; need for reform, 84
Language difficulties, 13–14, 111, 115, 136, 148–51
Lewis, Arthur, 110
Literacy, see Illiteracy
Loans, foreign, 29, 51, 67

Malaria, 15, 79–80, 82
Manpower Resources Division, 145, 177, 179
Manufacturing: output, 25, 26 (tab), 73; employment in, 71–74, 88; demand for trained manpower in, 74–75; growth, 74–75, 88, 152–53, 156; estimated demand vs. utilization in, 85; salary of skilled workers in, 91; capital requirements for expansion, 156–57
Menelik, Emperor, 13, 14
Military: government expenditures on, 34; civilian sector and development, 43; in school top-offs, 56, 57, 58
Ministry of Community Development, 160
Ministry of Economic Development, 174–75
Ministry of Education, 174–75

Ministry of Land Reform, 14
Ministry of National Community Development, 175, 176, 177, 179
Missionaries, 16–17
Mobility of labor force, 92–93, 147
Muslims, 16

National Manpower Advisory Committee, 176–79
Nurses, 81–82

Occupations: attitudes on, 16; labor force distribution by, 24, 71–73, 74, 88, 152–53, 156; estimated employment distribution by, 71–73, 74; of foreign population, 96, 97; of Alemaya graduates, 101–2; educational system related to, 114–16, 157
Organization for African Unity, 20

Peace Corps, 64, 65, 100, 128, 135
Physicians, 80–81, 82
Planning Board, 174
Population: topography and, 13–14; ratio with land, 15; characteristics, 21–22; growth, 70; projected growth rate, 74; health status of, 79–80; ratio of trained medical manpower to, 80–81, 82; characteristics of foreign, 95–96; percent enrolled in schools, 162

Revenues, see Government revenues
Roads, 17, 143; government and, 34; rural vs. urban, 84
Rural areas: manpower studies and, 7–8; population of, 15; health programs and, 17–18, 160; literacy in, 22–23, 32–33; opportunities, urban opportunities vs., 23, 33, 40, 42; occupational distribution of labor force, 24; school attendance in, 32–33; services in, 33; skilled manpower problems, 37, 77, 87, 147; community development projects, 77–78, 160–61, 166; educational expansion and, 112–13, 131, 156, 157–58; church

schools in, 113–14; economic development and, 113, 164–66; education and way of life in, 159, 160, 161, 163–66; unemployment and underemployment in, 160, 163–64; see also Agriculture

Salaries and wages: supply-demand and, 6–7, 32, 41; private vs. government, 77, 94, 98, 99; of college graduates, 40, 77, 91, 142; development objectives and structure of, 43; skill and, 91, 97–99, 154; of foreigners, 96–97; relations with productivity, 106; utilization alteration and, 106; gearing to education, 145–46; work level as criterion for, 146
Secondary schools: estimated enrollment, 53–54; alternatives for 10th grade students, 54; training institutions and, 54–58; drop-outs and top-offs from, 54–58; preparation of teachers, 63–66; educational expansion and, 111–12; curriculum guidelines, 114–16; per capita student costs in, 125; available teacher supply, 126; projected teacher need, 127–28, 129; enrollment in, 162
Skills: estimation of demand for, 2–3; shortages of, 2, 37; acquisition methods, 9, 69; rural vs. urban development of, 32–33; requirements for different, 38; salary and, 91, 97–99, 154; competence and, 106–7; economic planning and. 155
Students: foreign study by, 18, 19, 102–5, 144; commitments and incentives for education, 41–42, 137–39, 141, 149–50; ESLC and, 41, 52–53, 60; grade and age distribution of, 47–52; flow through secondary schools, 53–58; alternatives for 10th grade, 54; dropouts, 55, 56, 60, 61, 111; quality of university, 60, 66; medical, 80–81, 82; outflow controls, 104–5;

distribution in university departments, 120, 121–22; per capita cost of educating, 125; enrollment projections, 127–28; controlled flow of, 132; recommendations for stipends, 141–43

Teachers: available pool, 61–66, 79, 111, 112, 126–29, 135–36; foreign, 62–66, 100, 128, 135; preparation of, 62–66, 112; turnover of, 63, 100–1, 127, 128; university training program for, 64; demand for college graduates, 79; conflict with administration, 100, 101; disadvantages of profession, 100–1, 139–40, 141, 148–51; wage scale, 106; educational expansion and, 111, 112, 126–29; recommendations for university, 117–19; enrollment projections in determining need for, 127–28; standards for, 131–32; recommendations on training institutions for, 135–36; effective aids for, 136–37; bonding system for, 138–39, 140; career system for, 139, 140–41; need for data on, 170

Technical Institute at Bahar Dar, 18–19

Telecommunications, 35

Theodorus, Emperor, 13

Trained manpower: utilization problems, 37–39, 87–88; foreign vs. local, 39–40; commitments of, 41–42, 137–39, 141, 149–50; projected industrial growth and, 74–75; encouragement of, into rural areas, 87; government as employer, 88; salaries of, 91, 97–99; training programs in production of, 170–71

Trained manpower supply and demand, 70–89; estimates of future, 2–7, 84–86, 171, 172; salary and, 6–7, 32, 41; government expenditures and, 35; educational system planning and, 43, 119–22, 130–31,

132, 155–56, 157; for teachers, 61–66, 79, 111, 112; in manufacturing, 74–75; industrial growth and, 74–75, 88; changes in government, 76–79, 86–87; in health services, 79–83; in agriculture, 83–84; utilization and, 105; adjustment approaches, 153–54; need for data on, 168–69; foreigners and, 172

Training: alterations of flow into, 2; work level and, 5; in supply-demand estimation, 7, 32; competence related to, 8; Italians and, 17; system capacity, 36; effectiveness of system, 143–44; foreigners' role in, 144–45; formal apprenticeship system, 145; for community development projects, 161

Unemployment of rural population, 160, 163–64

University, 58–61; enrollment by faculty, 58–59; enrollment by grade, 58–60; enrollment policies, 60–61, 66, 116–17, 119–20, 121, 132; quality of students, 60, 66; teacher training, 64; two-year diploma program, 65, 117; foreign prototypes for, 67–69, 129–30; medical school, 80–81, 82; agriculture faculty, 83; recommendations on staff, 117–19; recommendations on curriculum, 117, 119, 120–21; Extension Division, 118–19; manpower criteria and planning, 119–22, 178; student distribution in departments, 120, 121–22; responsibilities and role, 122; cost of enrollment increases, 125; per capita student costs in, 125; relating capacity to number of students, 132

Urban areas: population of, 21–22, 163, 165; literacy in, 22, 32–33; occupational distribution of labor force, 24; quality of education in, 33; opportunities, rural op-

Urban areas (*Continued*)
portunities vs., 42; foreigners in, 96; unemployment of rural youth in, 163–64
USAID, 18, 34
Utilization of manpower, 9, 37–39, 90–108; government regulations and, 41–42, 137–39, 141, 149–50; incentives and, 43; in manufacturing, demand forecast vs., 85; distribution difficulties, 87–88; in Civil Service, 92–93; in nongovernment organizations, 94; of foreign skill in private sector, 94, 95–96; problems in education, 100–1; of Alemaya graduates, 101–2; foreign study and, 102–5; effect on supply, 105; potential for altering, 106; wage-productivity relations and, 106–7

Van Pischke, J. D., 28
Vocational and technical schools, 41; in topping-off secondary-school students, 54–58; enrollment in, 57; subsidized programs, 57–58; teacher availability for, 65; problems in developing, 68–69; agricultural, 83; curriculum planning for, 115–16; bonding system of, 138; data collection on, 170

Weber, Max, 11
Women: in population, 21, 22, 23; literacy of, 22, 23; opportunities in rural vs. urban areas, 42; increasing participation of, 164, 169
Wonji Sugar Estates, 20, 36
Work permits for foreigners, 96

Zach, Arnold, 85